# I FORGIVE, FOR MY SAKE

Apostle G. D. Numbere

**ISBN: 978-978-52114-1-2**



Unless otherwise stated, all Scripture quotations are from the King James Version of the Bible.

Published in 2014 by:
GREATER EVANGELISM PUBLICATIONS
47 Isiokpo Street D/Line, P. O. BOX 946, Port Harcourt
Rivers State, Nigeria, West Africa.
Tel:+2348182037449, +2347039886911, +2348176177088,
E-mail: gep@greaterevangelism.com
www.greaterevangelism.com
www.greaterevangelismuk.org

**PRINTED BY: Osia Digital Press**
#8 Owhonda Street, Diobu, P.H. R/S. Nigeria.
08033128938, 08037085272

BREAK THE JINX IN YOUR PERSONAL LIFE!

BREAK THE JINX IN YOUR FAMILY!

BREAK THE JINX IN THE CHURCH!

BREAK THE JINX IN SOCIETY!

BREAK THE JINX IN THE COMMUNITY!

BREAK THE JINX IN THE NATION!

"I FORGIVE, FOR MY SAKE"

↓

THE MASTER KEY!

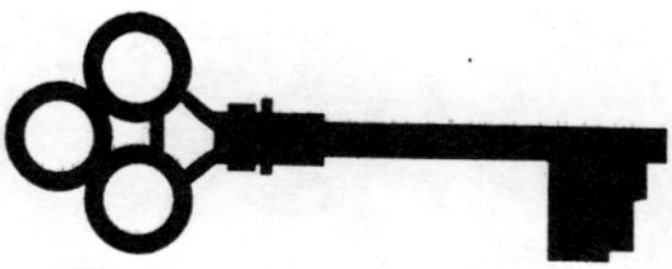

BREAK THE JINX IN YOUR PERSONAL LIFE!

BREAK THE JINX IN YOUR FAMILY!

BREAK THE JINX IN THE CHURCH!

BREAK THE JINX IN SOCIETY!

BREAK THE JINX IN THE COMMUNITY!

BREAK THE JINX IN THE NATION!

"I FORGIVE FOR MY SAKE"

THE MASTER KEY!

# DEDICATION

This book, **"I FORGIVE, FOR MY SAKE"** is dedicated to the Lord Jesus Christ, the Prince of Peace and the Prince of Life Who magnanimously forgave my sins and gloriously saved me on Sunday, 11th May 1969 in the Chapel on the campus of University of Ife (now Obafemi Awolowo), Ibadan Campus, Nigeria. *"Bless the Lord, O my soul: and all that is within me, bless his holy name... Who forgiveth all thine iniquities; who healeth all thy diseases; Who redeemeth thy life from destruction..."* (Psalms 103:1-4)

# ACKNOWLEDGEMENTS

I very sincerely acknowledge and I am immensely grateful for the contributions of members of my family and several other sincere friends of mine in faith.

1. PASTOR DR. NONYEM NUMBERE – MY WIFE AND MY EDITOR:

   For her marvellous contributions, devotion and commitment in seeing to it that this important book is published. She proof-read, corrected and re-corrected every sentence and every line.

2. TEACHER MRS. TAMUNONYE (TAMMY) EJIMADU:

   Tammy, a very smart computer guru churned out the pages faster than her mother and I could produce them and very accurately too! We did not have the drudgery of correcting and re-correcting typographical errors. Brilliant!

3. MY BROTHER MINISTERS

Who also proof read the manuscript, made their inputs by suggestions, corrections and comments. I refer particularly to –

i. Pastor Oluwafemi Martins who wrote the Foreword
ii. Professor Danny McCain (Department of Religion, University of Jos, Nigeria)
iii. Bishop Winston Iwo (Grace Covenant Ministries, Port Harcourt, Nigeria)
iv. Rev. Stephen Akinola (Redemption Ministries, Port Harcourt, Nigeria)
v. Pastor Belemina Obunge (Redeemed Christian Church of God, Rivers/Bayelsa Region, Nigeria).
vi. Rev. Moses Kumdam (Church of Christ In Nations, COCIN, Nigeria)

May the Almighty God bless all of them richly in Jesus Name.

# TABLE OF CONTENTS

# PREFACE

"UNFORGIVENESS" is a cankerworm that has eaten deep into the lives of individuals, in homes, in society as well as in the Church.

"UNFORGIVENESS" is a bait which Satan uses to trap people especially Christians.

The person who does not forgive finds himself or herself caught in a vicious web of anger, pain, bitterness, suspicion, terrible physical and spiritual afflictions that may even lead to death, now and in eternity.

There is no way of quantifying the damages "UNFORGIVENESS" does to man.

The Lord opened my eyes to see some of them and I began to preach the message on **"Forgiveness"** and **"Unforgiveness".** The Lord further impressed on my heart to **make** the subject of **"forgiveness" more personal.** That was why I arrived at the title, "I FORGIVE, FOR MY SAKE."

I discovered that from the time I began to preach on this new title, many more in my audience, home and abroad, began to appropriate "FORGIVENESS" and saw themselves as its first line of charge. They began to break loose by forgiving offenses and offenders no matter what, and their testimonies were outstanding and immediate!

Several of them specifically requested that I should write a book on the title, "I FORGIVE, FOR MY SAKE." God enabled me to do so and what you have in your hand is that title.

**"I FORGIVE, FOR MY SAKE"** is another way of highlighting the Lord's Prayer as taught in Matthew 6:12, "FORGIVE US OUR DEBTS, AS WE FORGIVE OUR DEBTORS."

I pray to God that as you patiently read through this book, the truths contained therein will bless you, bless your home, bless your church and **through you,** bless society in general.

Apostle G. D. Numbere

# FOREWORD

How do you feel when a father requests that you write the foreword to a book he wrote? For me, it was mixed feelings – joy, a sense of privilege and gratitude to God yet, there was a tinge of trepidation. However, when I eventually read through the manuscript, I was full of praises to God and was not surprised at the diligence of the author on the expository depth of the book.

Whoever truly wants to know the background, the beauty and the benefits of cultivating the spirit of forgiveness rather than experience the grave consequences of harboring an unforgiving spirit, then **"I Forgive, For My Sake"** is a must read. Apostle G. D. Numbere delved into the Pre-Law vengeance of 'seventy times seven' during the period of Cain and Lamech, the first two recorded murderers in creation history (Genesis Chapter 4), traced it to the Mosaic Era of Old Testament Law of 'Tit for Tat' (equality of vengeance, or 'an eye for an eye' in Leviticus 24:17-22) and masterfully ended with the mitigation of these two era of the Law to the Grace of Forgiveness and Love preached by our Lord and Saviour Jesus Christ (Matthew 5:38-39; Matthew 18:22 and Luke 17:3-4). Emphasizing this truth also with a recap of the story of Shylock and his demand for a pound of flesh confirms that as it is in the realm of the spiritual so it is in the secular.

The book **"I Forgive, For My Sake"** is indeed a sermon from the heart of a truly called Apostle of our Lord and Savior Jesus Christ. This is evident in the manner in which Apostle G. D. Numbere, the author, satisfied all departments that makes for a good sermon. **"I Forgive, For My Sake"** is a beautifully written sermon that will stand the test of time. The reason is simple – the book meets the criteria of every good sermon which must:

- **Interpret Scripture**. Apostle Numbere effectively interpreted Scripture in **"I Forgive, For My Sake"**. He demonstrated, each time he was quoting Scripture, a reliable connection between the author's and the original audience's understanding of a given text and his own contemporary interpretation which is again evident in his superb use of illustrations.

- **Inform** the mind. He also succeeded in making me and I dare say whoever reads **"I Forgive, For My Sake"**, know and understand something about God's truth as it affects forgiving one another as well as benefiting from the grace of divine forgiveness. This is the thrust of the book. What I think Apostle Numbere has done in **"I Forgive, For My Sake"** is to confirm that he is one of the few who know that the turning point between the darkness of the present age and the consummation of God's kingdom has come for the believer who operates in the power and efficacy of forgiveness.

I perceive Apostle Numbere has been led by the Holy Spirit to inform this generation to look toward the great reckoning which the world is approaching, the disclosure of God's majesty in the final judgment. Forgiveness is the one great gift of God bestowed on fallen man. In teaching the disciples to pray, Jesus was emphatic on this in Mark 11:25-26.

- **Instruct** the heart. Anyone reading **"I Forgive, For My Sake"** will discover that to avoid the reader taking emotional decisions, Apostle Numbere does not only inform the mind but ensures the heart is duly instructed.

- **Influence** behaviour. The essence of the Bible is to bring about behavioural change (2 Timothy 3:16-17). The cognitive, behavioural and affective impact of Scriptures. This runs through the twenty-one chapters of **"I Forgive, For My Sake"**. As it happened to me as I read through the manuscript, readers will most likely join the author in offering the prayer – "Lord, give me the grace to forgive".

In **"I Forgive, For My Sake"**, Apostle Numbere interprets Scripture, informs and instructs the mind and heart of those who will read the book for these are processes that naturally influence behavior. This means Apostle Numbere has been able to satisfy the needs of a good sermon through effective means of communication. Communication in this context means the connection between the preacher and the present audience's understanding of a text. He confirms himself as an effective communicator who exhibits the desire to bring passages of Scripture into contact with life through very realistic and meaningful illustrations – his own personal experience and the encounter with a woman in Rwanda.

The chapter titles are impacting, accurate and clear. Each precisely reveals the author's intention. The texts are properly introduced and stated. Introduction used in each chapter raises one need or the other and are tied to the main propositions ensuring that purpose is effectively stated whilst the body structures and conclusions are properly explained and applied.

Reading through **"I Forgive, For My Sake"** I realized God was speaking to me through the author and I am sure this will be the experience of anyone who reads the book. The book has the three basic essentials that should be found in a good book - **Information, Wide**

**Experience** and **Passion**. Apostle Numbere exhibits a passionate concern to preserve and promulgate the wholesome gospel of our Lord and Savior Jesus Christ.

If expository preaching is the communication of a biblical concept, derived from and transmitted through a historical, grammatical and literary study of a passage in its context, which the Holy Spirit first applies to the personality and experience of the preacher, and through the preacher, applies to the hearers (readers), then Apostle Numbere in the book **"I Forgive, For My Sake"** has proven he is an expository preacher par excellence. You will agree with me on this after reading his recap of two of his experiences – immediately after his new birth on May 11, 1969 and his encounter with Chief Mato. How one wished the life of Chief Mato did not end the way it was narrated in the book and that he did repent and became a beneficiary of the glory of God and the power of forgiveness.

I hereby wholeheartedly recommend the book **"I Forgive, For My Sake"** to you. It is a veritable treasure chest of information, practical advice and spiritual guidance. It will provoke, challenge, motivate, refresh and enlighten you.

I thank Daddy as the author is fondly called, for this singular honor of writing the foreword to this treasure chest titled **"I Forgive, For My Sake"**. In Jesus most merciful name, I pray God's grace of a forgiving spirit upon all who will read the book.

**Pastor Oluwafemi O. Martins**
Director, Communications and Development
West Africa Theological Seminary (WATS)
Ipaja, Lagos, Nigeria

# COMMENTS

In this searching, sound and strong book, Apostle G. D. Numbere compels us to our knees and to the theatre of the Holy Spirit – where our hearts and consciences are subjected to a thorough search, from the foundations of the basement to the roof.

For success with God does not reside in how far we travelled, how well we preached and to how many people etc. It does not rest in how many times we appeared on TV screens and certainly does not rest in what opinion the press and the world have of us.

**It rests in how clean we come out at the other end before God Almighty!**

To receive forgiveness from God or man is one thing – a wonderful, exciting, triumphant experience but to go from there and dispense the same forgiveness to others is ANOTHER!

To remain deeply wounded, troubled, affected and afflicted by an injury done or a wound passed by someone, somewhere and sometime ago is practical unforgiveness.

No matter what is done and inspite of the beaming smiles all around, the heart is festered with wounds and damages and the memory is twisted, tormented and tortured. To carry that to the grave is appalling.

David the son of Jesse, had greatly suffered in the hands of Shimei. In the day of Absalom's rebellion, Shimei cast dust upon David, ridiculed him and called him names. David's men wanted to react, but then David restrained them. When the kingdom returned to David, Shimei came trembling and prostrating for mercy. David ostensibly forgave him, **but that was a show of mercy designed to suit the occasion.** Shimei never knew that there was deep-seated animosity stored in the heart of David against him (2 Samuel 16:5 – 14; 19:15 – 23). Only when King David was handing over to Solomon his son did we hear him say:

(1 Kings 2:8 – 9)

> [8]*And, behold, thou hast with thee Shimei the son of Gera, a Benjamite of Bahurim, which cursed me with a grievous curse in the day when I went to Mahanaim: but he came down to meet me at Jordan,* ***and I sware to him by the Lord, saying, I will not put thee to death with the sword.***
> [9] *Now therefore hold him not guiltless: for thou art a wise man, and knowest what thou oughtest to do unto him; but his hoar head bring thou down to the grave with blood.*

This was speedily executed in 1 Kings 2:36 - 46. It is sad that at the close of David's life, when the curtains were to be drawn on him and he was to meet God, his heart was raging with vengeance against the man he had "forgiven" in time past. And he was busy teaching his son, his heir, the bitter paths of unforgiveness and **murder.**

When the cords of love rooted in the human heart, get "transformed" and become the tentacles of an octopus, fastening themselves on every victim in sight, the heart becomes a veritable chamber of horrors. God, save us from every root of unforgiveness!

Yes, for MY SAKE, I forgive!

**Stephen Akinola**
Senior Pastor
Redemption Ministries, Port Harcourt, Nigeria.

Apostle Numbere has in this remarkable book touched a salient topic that has hindered the blessings and stunted the spiritual growth of many people including notable ministers of the gospel.

The several illustrations, biblical references and outstanding testimonies mentioned in this book bring to light the subject matter and emphasize the need for forgiveness to be a lifestyle.

It will be difficult for a reader of this book to do otherwise. The impact is awesome.

The author has put to play his years of experience in ministry and without an iota of doubt, writes based on an exemplary life of forgiveness worthy of emulation.

As a father in the faith, Apostle Numbere has in his characteristic fatherly manner through the inspiration of the Holy Spirit provided a solution to as many that desire to be free from the cankerworm of unforgiveness that has affected and defiled the destiny of many.

We thank God for this gift. To Him be the glory.

**Pastor Belemina Obunge**
Pastor in Charge of Region
Redeemed Christian Church God
Rivers /Bayelsa , Nigeria.

Do you desire or really want to be in heaven? Do you desire or want good health? Do you desire or want long life full of blessings? And have you truly enjoyed God's forgiveness such that you are sure you are truly a Christian on your way to heaven?

Then, FORGIVENESS IS AN IMPERATIVE FOR YOU AND NEVER AN OPTION! This means that if you do not forgive all those who wrong you, YOU CANNOT BE IN HEAVEN. And even in this life, you will suffer various ill-health; you will not enjoy this life; thereafter end in HELL FIRE FOREVER AND EVER. Your lack of forgiving all who wrong you shows clearly you are not a Christian. This is because true Christians on their way to heaven have enjoyed God's forgiveness. Hence, they forgive just as God in Christ Jesus has forgiven them while they were still sinners on their way to eternal condemnation.

> *But God commendeth his love toward us, in that, while we were yet sinners, Christ died for us.*
> (Romans 5:8)
>
> *For the wages of sin is death; but the gift of God is eternal life through Jesus Christ our Lord.*
> (Romans 6:23)

This means, if you have truly enjoyed God's forgiveness, you must forgive all who wrong you, even if they do not ask you for forgiveness. More so, always beware that when you forgive, you are doing good to yourself and not actually the people you forgive. Lack of forgiveness means harming yourself. Find why and how in this book – **"I Forgive, For My Sake"**.

Brother/sister, if you read the testimonies of the Rwandan lady and the Liberian man in this book to mention just two; you have no good reason not to forgive whatever has been done to you. I am not sure your case is worse than theirs; but even if it is, only totally surrender to Jesus, and He will give you all you need to forgive and let go.

**To Apostle G. D. Numbere**: Thank God for letting God use you from your youthful age to date; to be a great blessing to Christendom! May God continue to increase you even in your old age until you hand over the MANTLE TO TRUSTWORTHY AND YOUNG CHRISTIANS TO CONTINUE YOUR GOOD WORKS (2 Timothy 2:2); UNTIL OUR SAVIOUR AND LORD, JESUS CHRIST COMES TO TAKE US HOME IN JESUS' NAME. AMEN AND AMEN!! **CHEERS & BRAVO DADDY!!!**

Continue until you say like the great Apostle Paul in 2 Timothy 4:7–8 at God's appointed time, *"I have fought the good fight, I have finished the race, I have kept the faith. Now there is in store for me the crown of righteousness, which the Lord, the righteous judge will award to me on that day and not only to me, but also to all who have longed for his appearing".*(NIV).

Daddy, thanks very much for the underserved honour, for the privilege to read this before it is printed for public consumption. I feel highly humbled and elated. I am indeed grateful sir!!!

**Rev. Moses Sati Kumdam**
Administrative & Estate Officer
Church Of Christ In Nations (COCIN) Headquarters
Jos, Plateau State, Nigeria

Forgiveness is a virtue that is a scarce commodity with majority of human beings, many of them in Church. It is one attribute of God that man has the least inclination to display easily. Man is prepared to love, sometimes extraordinarily. He is prepared to live in peace and sometimes seeks it with passion. But forgiveness seems a task that cannot be easily accomplished. Yet forgiveness is a command from God.

To forgive those who offend you, in its true sense, is for the benefit of the one showing forgiveness.
(Matthew 6:14, 15 – NKJV)

> 14 *For if you forgive men their trespasses, your heavenly Father will also forgive you.*
> 15 *But if you do not forgive men their trespasses, neither will your Father forgive your trespasses.*

In this book, **"I Forgive, For My Sake"**, Apostle G. D. Numbere has spared no effort in espousing the significance of forgiveness, the dangers of unforgiveness and the benefits of freely forgiving whoever offends us from scriptural and experiential standpoints. It simplifies the subject of forgiveness and makes it attractive and easy to understand. You will love it.

**Rt. Rev. Winston T. Iwo**
Presiding Bishop
Grace Covenant Ministries
Port Harcourt, Nigeria.

A book on forgiveness may be one of the most strategic things that the Church needs today. Many of our churches are caught up in power and prosperity and so many other things to the point that we have often neglected the "weightier" issues in the Scripture. Forgiveness is so fundamental. I am grateful that the author followed the leadership of the Lord in writing this book. I pray that many people will read it and be blessed and convicted by it.

I never cease to be amazed at my good friend, Apostle Geoffrey Numbere. When he sent me a draft copy of this book, I was amazed by several things. First, I am amazed at how often Apostle Numbere is on target in contemporary issues that affect his community and nation. As I think about the Church in Nigeria, I am not sure that there is a more important topic that the Church needs to address than forgiveness. There are millions of offended people in Nigeria. Conflicts abound on every hand. We have inter-personal conflicts; we have conflicts in the church; we have inter-ethnic conflicts; we have political conflicts; we have religious conflicts. We have conflicts between the unions and businesses; we have conflicts between the herders and the farmers; we have conflict between the fishermen and the oil industry; we have conflicts between the elders and the youth; we even have conflicts between the men and the women. Every one of those conflicts leads to offenses. And every one of those offenses leads to bitterness, anger, resentment, unkind words, separation and sometimes even violence. The only way to resolve all of these conflicts is for all involved to simply forgive and move forward. Yes, there is the issue of justice. Any reasonable person would not want people to do wicked things and then escape justice. However, three different times in this book, Apostle Numbere reminds us of a very important truth: *"...Vengeance is mine; I will repay, saith the Lord"* (Romans 12:19). The Bible says that the State must uphold justice and does not necessarily have to forgive sins against the State (Romans 13:2-4) but we as individuals must learn to forgive and leave justice up to God and the State. So a big thank you to Apostle Numbere for discerning the need of the day and articulating the Biblical answer so forcefully.

The second thing that amazes me about Apostle Numbere is the method he used in this book. I teach my students who are pursuing a Masters Degree (Master of Arts – MA) in New Testament what we call the "Biblical Theological Method". In this method, if we are looking at a theme like forgiveness, my students go through the Bible and find everything in the Bible about that theme. They study those passages in their context and then extract the relevant truths about that subject from each of these passages. Next, they organize that material and present it in a written readable manner. This is tedious work and when they finish, they have often only discovered what they already knew in a general way. However, once a student has used the Biblical Theological Method correctly, he or she should have a good understanding of the meaning of that particular topic in the Bible. Although he has never studied in a seminary, I am quite amazed at how closely Apostle Numbere followed this methodology in writing this book. All of the points he makes in this book are extracted naturally from a particular scripture. He does not read into the passage that which is not there and he does not omit things that are there. When you do this kind of research, you are on pretty solid theological ground.

The third thing that amazes me about Apostle Numbere is how hard he works. This is a man who is past retirement age according to the Federal Government. However, he is still working hard to make sure he addresses the contemporary needs of the Church and society. When I lived in Port Harcourt, Nigeria, about 23 years ago, I walked into his office one day and was surprised. I had known Apostle Numbere as a dynamic extemporaneous speaker, a front line evangelist and an uncompromising church leader. However, what I saw in his office was a desk that was piled high with ten or twelve open books. I asked him what he was doing and he said that he was "studying for a sermon." That scattered my view of an apostle. I thought that such people spent much time in prayer and depended upon the Holy Spirit to give them what they were to say as they were speaking. However, Apostle Numbere taught me that day that he was a man who believed in working, in studying, in searching out truth from the Word of God and organizing it in a coherent manner. This book on forgiveness illustrates very clearly that work ethic. It took time to discover all these scriptures related to forgiveness, study them in their context, extract the key truths and then organize all of this together. This book was not just written spontaneously off the top of his head. As an author of several books myself, it is very obvious to me that this book grew out of hours and days of old-fashioned tedious hard work.

There is one more thing that amazes me about Apostle Numbere and that is his amazing ability to communicate. The very first thing that impressed me about this man was his communication ability. And there was one particular thing that got my attention. Apostle Numbere was the first major Nigerian preacher I met who used an almost exclusive African style of communication. There was no attempt on his part to imitate the American Pentecostal preachers as some preachers did. He was himself when he preached and since he was an African that meant his preaching had a distinct African flavor. It is almost impossible to reproduce on paper the words and style of a preacher on the pulpit. However, if I close my eyes after reading some of these sentences in this book, I can almost see the apostle pacing up and down on the pulpit and I can clearly hear vintage Numbere speaking to us from the pages of this book. And the good thing about this kind of preaching is that you can hear these sermons over and over again as you read the book over and over again.

For these and other reasons I am happy to commend this passionate call for forgiveness to the Christian community. Anyone who reads and follows the advice found in this book will be closer to heaven as a result.

**Prof Danny McCain**
Department of Religion and Philosophy
Faculty of Arts, University of Jos, Nigeria.

# CHAPTER 1

# FORGIVENESS: AN INITIATIVE OF GOD

A man has had a very frustrating day at his work place. He comes home tired and irritated because of all the pressures of his job. His attitude causes him to shout at his wife, making her feel offended. If you were a friend of the family and happened to be there that day, who would you encourage to initiate the reconciliation – the husband who committed the offence or the wife who was offended? You would probably encourage the husband to seek his wife's forgiveness. However, in the Bible we discover a most amazing truth. We learn that God, the one who has been offended, is actually the one who initiates the reconciliation!

The Bible narrates this scenario to us:

> *For all have sinned, and come short of the glory of God;* (Romans 3:23). This means all

human beings have sinned against God.

*For the wages of sin is death...* (Romans 6:23);

This means that those who sin will die.

However, God, not willing that any should perish, initiated a scheme, a design to forgive our sins and to cleanse us from all unrighteousness. And that Way, that means of forgiving our sins, is His only begotten Son, Jesus Christ.

*For God so loved the world, that he gave his only begotten Son, that whosoever believeth in him should not perish, but have everlasting life.* (John 3:16)

*He that believeth on the Son hath everlasting life: and he that believeth not the Son shall not see life; but the wrath of God abideth on him.* (John 3:36)

If God did not fashion a plan to forgive sins, we would all have perished.

(Psalms 130:3 – 4)

3 *If thou, Lord, shouldest mark iniquities, O Lord, who shall stand?*

4 *But there is forgiveness with thee, that thou mayest be feared.*

He gave His Son to forgive our sins.

(Colossians 1:13 – 14)

> [13] *Who hath delivered us from the power of darkness, and hath translated us into the kingdom of his dear Son:*
>
> [14] *In whom we have redemption through his blood, even the forgiveness of sins:*

(Romans 6:23)

> *...the gift of God is eternal life through Jesus Christ our Lord.*

(1 John 1:8 – 9)

> [8] *If we say that we have no sin, we deceive ourselves, and the truth is not in us.*
>
> [9] *If we confess our sins, he is faithful and just to forgive us our sins, and to cleanse us from all unrighteousness.*

Thus, God Himself is the initiator of forgiveness. If this is what He Himself does, He certainly expects all men to do as He did; to follow His example and forgive sins, offences and wrongs done us.

# CHAPTER 2

# FORGIVENESS: THE PARABLE OF THE UNFORGIVING SERVANT

(Matthew 18: 21-35)

21 *Then came Peter to him, and said, Lord, how oft shall my brother sin against me, and I forgive him? till seven times?*

22 *Jesus saith unto him, I say not unto thee, Until seven times: but, Until seventy times seven.*

23 *Therefore is the kingdom of heaven likened unto a certain king, which would take account of his servants.*

24 *And when he had begun to reckon, one was brought unto him, which owed him ten thousand talents.*

25 *But forasmuch as he had not to pay, his lord commanded* ***him*** *to be sold, and* ***his wife****, and* ***children****, and* ***all that he had****, and payment to be made.*

*26 The servant therefore fell down, and worshipped him, saying, Lord, have patience with me, and I will pay thee all.*
*27 Then the lord of that servant was moved with compassion, and loosed him, and forgave him the debt.*
*28 But the same servant went out, and found one of his fellowservants, which owed him an hundred pence: and he laid hands on him, and took him by the throat, saying, Pay me that thou owest.*
*29 And his fellowservant fell down at his feet, and besought him, saying, Have patience with me, and I will pay thee all.*
*30 And he would not: but went and cast him into prison, till he should pay the debt.*
*31 So when his fellowservants saw what was done, they were very sorry, and came and told unto their lord all that was done.*
*32 Then his lord, after that he had called him, said unto him, O thou wicked servant, I forgave thee all that debt, because thou desiredst me:*
*33 Shouldest not thou also have had compassion on thy fellowservant, even as I had pity on thee?*

*34 And his lord was wroth, and delivered him to the tormentors, till he should pay all that was due unto him.*
*35 So likewise shall my heavenly Father do also unto you, if ye from your hearts forgive not every one his brother their trespasses.*

This parable, though talking about money owed, is actually about forgiveness. A parable is a short story that teaches a moral or spiritual lesson especially those told by Jesus Christ.

This particular parable explains one of the conditions required to enter the Kingdom of heaven. That is why Jesus started this parable with the statement: *"Therefore is the kingdom of heaven likened unto a certain king..."* and He ended with *"So likewise shall my heavenly Father do also unto you, if ye from your hearts forgive not everyone his brother their trespasses."*

The parable begins with a king who called his servants to give account. One of them owed him ten thousand talents but was unable to pay. This servant fell down at his master's feet and pleaded for forgiveness and his master forgave him all of his debts.

FORGIVENESS – A DEBT WE OWE

All of us like this servant, owe God. Every one of us is a debtor. We owe God for our sins; we owe Him for all the benefits He gives us daily such as the air we have been breathing right from birth. David cried,

> *What shall I render unto the Lord for all His benefits toward me?* (Psalms 116:12)

We all have debts we owe God which we cannot pay. The master said, "Pay me what you owe me!" But the servant could not pay. What he did was to fall down before his master and ask for forgiveness. That is exactly what we all must do. We are to go before the Lord, prostrate before Him and say, "God forgive me." We must be humble and heart broken when doing so for *"A broken and contrite heart He will not despise."* (Psalms 51:17 - paraphrased).

We are told that as he pleaded for mercy, his master forgave him (Verses 26, 27).

The scenario with his master repeated itself when he

met his own debtor. This same man had someone who was indebted to him for a lesser amount. His debtor pleaded with him for mercy and forgiveness but he would not forgive (Verse 28 – 30).

One of the greatest obstacles in the life of a child of God, an obstacle that stands between us and God, is unforgiveness.

FORGIVENESS, THE FIRST LESSON THE HOLY SPIRIT TAUGHT ME

In 1969, I was a young student studying Geology at the University of Ife (now Obafemi Awolowo University) Ibadan Campus, Nigeria when on Sunday, 11th May that year, a young man came that day to preach in the Chapel service. Though I was a terrible sinner, I loved going to church. The young preacher was not a regular priest but the Travelling Secretary of Scripture Union Nigeria, by name Brother (now Rev. Dr.) Mike Oye.

His testimonial sermon about his salvation convicted

me heavily of my sins. So I resolved not to leave the Chapel that day until I met with the Jesus that preacher was talking about. I went to see Rev. Oye after the service in the Vestry. The burden for the guilt of my sins was so heavy on me I slumped over a stool that was near me. As I was weeping, suddenly a gigantic opaque screen whose dimensions were undeterminable dropped in front of me. The height reached from heaven to earth and the width spanned from the east to the west. That dark screen had written on it, all the sins I had committed in my life time including my Bible, a looted article by my relative during the Nigerian Civil war! I wept and wept as I saw that list and then I shouted "IT IS TOO MUCH!" As soon as I screamed, an unseen hand came and ripped the screen from top to bottom and rolled back half to the east and half to the west and a bright light, brighter than the sun, shorn into my soul! All my guilt and sorrow vanished and with tears of joy, I began to shout, "I AM SAVED! I AM SAVED!" At the same time, I was baptized by the Holy Ghost with that bright light.

Meanwhile, Rev. Mike Oye realizing that the Lord was

dealing with me, had stopped praying and had stood by, just watching me. As I got up from my knees in tears still shouting, "I AM SAVED, I AM SAVED, he rushed to me and we hugged each other, he also weeping out of joy and our tears poured on each other's face.

I was led by the Holy Spirit to flip open a Bible on a nearby stool to Psalms 16 with emphasis on Verse 6: *"The lines are fallen unto me in pleasant places; yea, I have a goodly heritage."*

By this time it was lunchtime and the students had already gone to the dining hall. I left Rev. Mike Oye and in that joy and new spirit, ran across the field with all my strength to the dining hall. Though it was lunchtime, I was not going there to eat. No, my stomach was too full for lunch. There was an urgency in my spirit to do something much more important than eating. I had been a young man whose heart was so hard and so chronically unforgiving that I had many whom I had labelled as "enemies". I could never forget or forgive an offence or offender. My heart was like a blotting paper or sponge, soaking in, absorbing, retaining and remembering every little wrong done to me. But now, although nobody had taught me anything about forgiveness, I knew I had to forgive all who had offended me. I had not yet known any word of Scripture but it was the first lesson the Holy Spirit taught me. I could not retain anybody's sins any longer, no, not after God had forgiven all those sins recorded against me which I had seen written on that giant black screen. I needed to make peace with all my enemies.

The Holy Spirit led me into obedience. In the dining hall, I went from table to table, seeking out those I had offended and those who had offended me and I made peace with all of them. I told each and every one of them, "Please forgive me, I also forgive you."

Some of them had not really offended me, I had just disliked them at sight and for no just reason. Yes, sometimes you may find yourself disliking certain persons at first sight without their knowing. You dislike them either because of their appearance, carriage, manner of speaking or certain advantages they have which you do not have etc. You find yourself disliking them, being cold toward them, and all along they do not know what offence(s) they had committed that caused you to adopt such an attitude towards them. When you find yourself in such situations, do as I did, go to them, bare your heart to them and ask them to forgive you.

A number of them did not even remember that they had had any misunderstanding with me, but my heart was a repertoire of past events. I reminded such people of the date, the time and the details of their disagreement. I had never forgiven or forgotten, but that day was a different day. I had become a new man: *"Therefore if any man be in Christ, he is a new creature: old things are passed away; behold, all things are become new."* (2 Corinthians 5:17)

FORGIVENESS was the **first lesson** the Holy Spirit taught me! As I was forgiven **all** of my sins, so I forgave **all** that had offended me.

# CHAPTER 3

# THE SIN OF UNFORGIVENESS AND ITS IMPLICATIONS

There are three grave consequences for committing the sin of unforgiveness. Two of these are personal, followed by a third – retributive justice for family and business.

## 1. Personal Consequence: "In Chains and In Bondage"

There is a veiled truth in Verse 27 of Matthew 18, a truth not expressed directly and clearly. It states,

> *Then the lord of that servant was moved with compassion, and loosed him, and forgave him the debt."* (Matthew 18:27)

"LOOSED"

We find the same word "LOOSED" used in the story of Shadrach, Meshach and Abednego, the three faithful Jews thrown into a burning fiery furnace in Babylon by King Nebuchadnezzar. The king declared,

> *...Lo, I see four men loose, walking in the midst of the fire, and they have no hurt; and the form of the fourth is like the Son of God.* (Daniel 3:25)

King Nebuchadnezzar in astonishment asked his counsellors this question,

> *...Did not we cast three men bound into the midst of the fire?...* (Daniel 3:24)

Shedrach, Meshach and Abednego were bound by Nebuchadnezzar and thrown into the fiery furnace but loosed by God to walk free. We loose that which is bound. So when we read in Matthew 18:27 that the unforgiving servant was "loosed" it meant he was bound, he was chained and now loosed.

IN CHAINS

In the story of Peter in prison (Acts 12:6 – 12) when the angel of the Lord arrived, we read in Verse 7,

> *And, behold, the angel of the Lord came upon him, and a light shined in the prison: and he*

> *smote Peter on the side, and raised him up, saying, Arise up quickly. And his chains fell off from his hands.* (Acts 12:7)

Meaning, Peter's hands were loosed. In the preceding Verse, *"...Peter was sleeping between two soldiers, bound with two chains..."* (Acts 12:6). Thus, in every case we met the word "loosed" it meant something had been bound or chained. So was this unforgiving servant, he was bound and chained but was loosed when his master pardoned him.

IMPLICATIONS OF BEING BOUND OR CHAINED

There are several implications for being bound or chained. The first of which is that "movement is restricted." The second is that there is "no means of escape" for example a dog is chained up for a walk so it cannot escape.

Who restricted the movement of this unforgiving servant? Who chained him up? The Lord did! In Matthew 18:35 we read, *"So likewise shall my heavenly Father do also unto you, if ye from your hearts forgive not every one his brother their trespasses."*

I will leave the reader to fill in the details of what is involved when "movement is restricted" and when a man is "chained up."

But more frightening is the statement the Lord made, *"Verily I say unto thee, thou shalt by no means come out thence, till thou hast paid the uttermost farthing."* (Matthew 5:26)

TWO issues are involved here:

I. **"Thou shall by no means come out thence."** This means there will be no means of setting the unforgiving person free from that chain, that bondage. This means there will be no human solution to all the problems to be encountered. Prayers and fasting will not help; doctors and medications will bring no solution – "by no means" is the sentence! Even God Himself will not bring solution! So which is the way out? Just one and only one way.

ii. **"Till thou hast paid the uttermost farthing."** That one way is, pay all the debt to the uttermost farthing! That means to forgive to the last dreg of offense!!

Forgiveness is a debt we owe. That being so, the one solution we have for our total freedom is to **forgive all, everybody** (Matthew 18:35) **and every offense** (Matthew 5:25). And it is only when we have done so, will the order be given, by the Lord Himself, "Loose him", "set him free and let him go." (Matthew 18:27).

May God open our eyes to see the subject of our bondage.

**2. Personal Consequence: "Thrown to Tormentors"**

(Matthew 18:28-30)

> 28 *But the same servant went out, and found one of his fellow servants, which owed him an hundred pence: and he laid hands on him, and took him by the throat, saying, pay me that thou owest.*
>
> 29 *And his fellow servant fell down at his feet, and besought him, saying, Have patience with me, and I will pay thee all.*

> 30*And he would not: but went and cast him into prison, till he should pay the debt.*

This same servant went out after he had been pardoned and saw another person who owed him just a small amount of money. He held him by the throat saying, "Today you must pay me"! The debtor fell down and pleaded, "Please forgive me, I will pay you all later." But the servant refused, he said "You will pay me now and you will pay me all the money you owe me"! He beat him, slapped him and tormented him.

When the news got to the master, he sent for him, "This is what I heard about you my servant, is it true? After forgiving your huge debt, you could not forgive a man who owed you much less? You are wicked." For this, he delivered this man to the tormentors:

> *And his lord was wroth, and delivered him to the **tormentors,** till he should **pay all** that was due unto him.* (Verse 34)

A "tormentor" is something or a person who causes somebody to suffer.

Every sickness, every disease is a tormentor; every affliction is a tormentor. Tormentors keep us uncomfortable, they cause **pain** and they cause **anguish**. For example, the following are all tormentors:

1. Arthritis
2. Asthma
3. Cancer
4. Diabetes
5. Fever
6. Heart Disease
7. Hypertension
8. Infertility
9. Insomnia
10. Kidney Disease
11. Liver Disease
12. Mental Disorder
13. Migraine
14. Multiple Misfortunes
15. Skin Disease
16. Stomach Disorder
17. Urinary Disease etc

**A person who does not forgive attracts to himself one "tormentor" or the other.** For an illustration let us say you are unable to forgive someone. For that one person, you are afflicted with arthritis. For a second person you do not forgive, you add asthma to your arthritis; for a third person you won't forgive, you add cancer and the list goes on and on.

Is it any wonder that we always have one affliction after another? Today it is headache; tomorrow - stomach pains; the next day, "Urinary disease", the next, "Oh, I can't sleep!" etc. etc. "What is happening?" you ask. What is happening is that you have been thrown to "tormentors" and they will torment you until you learn to forgive men their trespasses against you. The more the people that you refuse to forgive, the more tormentors you attract to yourself.

### 3a. Retributive Justice for Family and Business

*But forasmuch as he had not to pay, his lord commanded him to be sold, and his wife, and children, and all that he had, and payment to be made.* (Verse 25)

There were grave personal consequences to this man. But besides him, the consequences also affected his family and his business. He and his family were "sold" in this order:

- The man
- His wife
- His children
- His property (business) – so payment could be made

I want us to learn this lesson. His wife was not there when he borrowed the money; his children were not there when he borrowed the money. Fathers, mothers, brothers, sisters, **what you do or fail to do does not begin and end with you; the consequences reach out to all the people and things that are dear to you!** This is illustrated in several portions of Scripture from the Old Testament to the New Testament.

- In the Law

  *Thou shalt not bow down thyself to them, nor serve them: for I the Lord thy God am a jealous God, visiting the iniquity of the fathers upon the children unto the third and fourth generation of them that hate me;* (Exodus 20:5)

- God's judgment on David
  *Now therefore the sword shall never depart from thine house; because thou hast despised me, and hast taken the wife of Uriah the Hittite to be thy wife.* (2 Samuel 12:10)

- Jesus to the Scribes and Pharisees
  *That upon you may come all the righteous blood shed upon the earth, from the blood of righteous Abel unto the blood of Zacharias son of Barachias, whom ye slew between the temple and the altar.* (Matthew 23:35)

- The testimony of Pilate's wife
  *When he was set down on the judgment seat, his wife sent unto him, saying, Have thou nothing to do with that just man: for I have suffered many things this day in a dream because of him.* (Matthew 27:19).
- The Jews

*Then answered all the people, and said, His blood be on us, and on our children.* (Matthew 27:25).

This statement was fulfilled in A.D. 70 when General Titus of Rome overwhelmed Jerusalem; crucified five hundred Jews every day on trees which lined the streets and torched the corpses so that they burned as street lights etc.

**b. Retributive Justice on Church Congregation**

As unforgiveness affects the individual, the family and business, so it affects the Church we belong to. There is a network effect.

This is how it works:

When one member fails to forgive another member in the Church, friends and relatives in the Church (if any) of the unforgiving person are affected by the same principle of the story of the unforgiving servant. Now, if there is a second unforgiving member, his or her friends and relatives in the Church (if any), are also affected negatively; and pretty soon the whole church is affected and netted and the blessings and progress of the Church are retarded. The Bible clearly teaches that,

> *...none of us liveth to himself, and no man dieth to himself.* (Romans 14:7); *...we are members one of another.* (Ephesians 4:25); *...there should be no schism in the body; but that the members should have the same care one for another.* (1 Corinthians 12:25) and, *...whether one member suffer, all the members suffer with it; or one member be honoured, all the members rejoice with it.* (1 Corinthians 12:26)

It is pertinent to state again, that forgiveness is a debt that we owe.

This parable tells us that much,

(Matthew 18: 25, 35)

> 25 *But forasmuch as he* ***had not to pay****, his lord commanded him to be sold, and his wife, and children, and all that he had, and* ***payment*** *to be made.*
>
> 35 *So likewise shall my heavenly Father do also unto you, if ye* ***from your hearts*** *forgive not every one his brother their trespasses.*

The Bible says, this servant would not forgive and so was thrown to tormentors till he would pay his debts. These tormentors will torment you until you pay all your debts meaning, **until** you forgive everybody from your heart!

INABILITY TO RETAIN GOD'S PARDON, GOD'S FORGIVENESS

Why was a man who was initially forgiven, pardoned and set free (Verse 27), back in bondage and thrown to tormentors to be tormented? Because of unforgiveness! Unforgiveness makes a man incapable of retaining God's pardon and forgiveness. The unforgiving servant lost his forgiveness and lost his freedom.

> *Whoso stoppeth his ears at the cry of the poor, he also shall cry himself, but shall not be heard.* (Proverbs 21:13)
>
> *Therefore it is come to pass, that as he cried, and they would not hear; so they cried, and I would not hear, saith the Lord of hosts* (Zechariah 7:13)

## THERE IS NO OTHER REMEDY

Problems and afflictions coming to us as a result of unforgiveness do not respond to doctor's cure; injections and tablets are ineffective neither will prayers avail no matter how hard we pray. So-called "dangerous prayers" will not bring any solution. Prayers like, "All you mammy water dancers, all you (whoever or whatever you call) die by fire, die by fire, fire, fire, be roasted, be roasted! Return to sender, return to sender, return to sender!" and all that. Nothing will roast, and nothing will die. The "returning", like a boomerang, will return to afflict you. David had prayed, *"Let the words of my mouth, and the meditation of my heart, be acceptable in thy sight, O Lord, my strength and my redeemer."* (Psalms 19:14) Now, those curse words you have spoken are they acceptable in God's sight? Those bitter thoughts in your heart are they acceptable in God's sight? Ask yourself. Think, beloved, think!

Now, some people go to some so-called Churches where the leaders always bias and poison their minds against somebody through spurious visions, dreams and prophecies. "Somebody" has done this; it is your husband that did this; it is your wife; it is your neighbour, it is a member of your family etc. etc," they are told. On hearing this, their mind is poisoned against that person. The result is that all over the place they have people they hold suspect – in their compound, in their home, in their office, their relatives, their maids etc. Everybody wants to harm or kill them; and with this, they move and live with an unforgiving spirit. Many friendships, relationships and even marriages have been broken or soured as a result of such spurious, false visions, dreams and prophecies. Unknown to them, these pastors are teaching them to be unforgiving and to be hateful. Thus, instead of setting them free as they promise, they make them enter into deeper bondage and troubles. Rather than solve their problems, they cause them to have even more problems than they had before and thus make them more miserable and confused. Not one problem of theirs will be solved this way because they have been thrown to "tormentors."

*Fools make mockery of sin.* (Proverbs 14:9-paraphrased) Be warned.

This servant is the same one that was forgiven and set free earlier but he is now again sentenced,

> *And his lord was wroth, and delivered him to the tormentors, till he should pay all that was due unto him.* (Matthew 18:34)

He is back into bondage! Why? Because he could not forgive – back into trouble, more trouble, because he could not forgive! You cannot live in unforgiveness and live a free, peaceful life, my friend; such are *"in the gall of bitterness and in the bond of iniquity."* (Acts 8:23). Paul describes such a state of animosity very aptly in (Romans 3:13 – 18)

> 13 *Their throat is an open sepulchre; with their tongues they have used deceit; the poison of asps is under their lips:*
> 14 *Whose mouth is full of cursing and bitterness:*
> 15 *Their feet are swift to shed blood:*
> 16 *Destruction and misery are in their ways:*
> 17 *And the way of peace have they not known:*
> 18 *There is no fear of God before their eyes.*

TWO LESSONS TO BE LEARNED

First, it is **not** the devil or an enemy or anyone else that will throw you into prison and to the "tormentors" but the Lord Himself will order it.

(Matthew 18:34)

> *And his lord was wroth, and delivered him to the tormentors...*

(Matthew 6:14 – 15)

> [14] *For if ye forgive men their trespasses, your heavenly Father will also forgive you:*
> [15] *But if ye forgive not men their trespasses, neither will your Father forgive your trespasses.*

Second, no other remedy, only total forgiveness will bring relief.

> ***...till he should pay all that was due unto him.*** (Matthew 18:34b)

DISASTER

At the end of the day, this unforgiving man's entire life was a total disaster. First, he was chained and kept in bondage. Second, he was thrown to "tormentors" and third, his family and business were ruined.

> *So likewise shall my heavenly Father do also unto you, if ye from your hearts forgive not everyone his brother their trespasses.* (Matthew 18:35)

# CHAPTER 4

# DEFILEMENT

Unforgiveness defiles a man.

"Defilement" means, "pollution". "To defile" means, "to corrupt the purity or perfection of something" (Webster's dictionary). For example, when fresh fish or meat gets rotten, it is defiled; it stinks just as dead bodies (corpses).

There is **physical** defilement and there is **spiritual** defilement. In St. Matthew's gospel, Jesus was teaching on spiritual defilement.
(Matthew 15:10 – 20)

> 10 *And he called the multitude, and said unto them, Hear, and understand:*
> 11 *Not that which goeth into the mouth defileth a man; but that which cometh out of the mouth, this defileth a man.*
> 12 *Then came his disciples, and said unto him, Knowest thou that the Pharisees were offended, after they heard this saying?*

*13 But he answered and said, Every plant, which my heavenly Father hath not planted, shall be rooted up.*
*14 Let them alone: they be blind leaders of the blind. And if the blind lead the blind, both shall fall into the ditch.*
*15 Then answered Peter and said unto him, Declare unto us this parable.*
*16 And Jesus said, Are ye also yet without understanding?*
*17 Do not ye yet understand, that whatsoever entereth in at the mouth goeth into the belly, and is cast out into the draught?*
*18 But those things which proceed out of the mouth come forth from the heart; and they defile the man.*
*19 For out of the heart proceed evil thoughts, murders, adulteries, fornications, thefts, false witness, blasphemies:*
*20 These are the things which defile a man: but to eat with unwashen hands defileth not a man.*

In Verse eleven He taught, "*Not that which goeth into the mouth defileth a man; but that which cometh out of the mouth, this defileth a man.*"

Explaining He said, *"But those things which proceed out of the mouth come forth from the heart; and they defile the man."* (Verse 18)

Explaining further, Jesus proceeded to name those things which come forth from the heart, which the mouth speaks (Verse 19), *For out of the heart proceed*

1. *Evil thoughts*
2. *Murders*
3. *Adulteries*
4. *Fornications*
5. *Thefts*
6. *False witness*
7. *Blasphemies*

And in Verse 20 He concluded, ***"These are the things which defile a man..."***

When a man's heart is defiled or polluted, he is a stinking moving corpse *"...is dead while she liveth"* (1 Timothy 5:6). It will make no difference what he puts on his physical body – silver, gold or diamonds; it will make no difference what perfume he or she daubs on the body. Spiritually, he or she is like a stinking corpse before God. He is defiled; she is defiled.

AN IMPEDIMENT TO THE BAPTISM OF THE HOLY SPIRIT (WHY THE CHURCH IS NOT REVIVED)

The Church is revived or will be revived only when the Holy Spirit baptizes her. When she (the Church) is polluted in heart against one another, hating, cursing and harboring bitterness in their hearts against one another, the Holy Spirit is prevented from falling on the Church. For as His Name is, so is He – HOLY! That way we become a burden, indeed a curse, on the Church instead of being a blessing. This is why it is urgent, very urgent that we *"purge out the old leaven of malice and wickedness that we may be a new lump."* (1 Corinthians 5:7 – 8- paraphrased), if we should be a blessing, an asset to the Church. It is even for our own personal good and benefit to do so because God warns,

(1 Corinthians 3:16 – 17)

> 16 *Know ye not that ye are the temple of God, and that the Spirit of God dwelleth in you?*
> 17 *If any man defile the temple of God, him shall God destroy; for the temple of God is holy, which temple ye are.*

# CHAPTER 5

# MORE IMPLICATIONS OF THE SIN OF UNFORGIVENESS

In addition to what we read in Chapter Three, there are amongst others, eight terrible consequences that one will face for failing to forgive.

### 1. Grieving the Holy Spirit

If you do not forgive, you will grieve the Holy Spirit. (Ephesians 4:29 – 32)

> [29]*Let no corrupt communication proceed out of your mouth, but that which is good to the use of edifying, that it may minister grace unto the hearers.*
>
> [30] *And grieve not the Holy Spirit of God, whereby ye are sealed unto the day of redemption.*
>
> [31] *Let all bitterness, and wrath, and anger, and clamour, and evil speaking, be put away from you, with all malice:*
>
> [32] *And be ye kind one to another, tenderhearted,*

*forgiving one another, even as God for Christ's sake hath forgiven you.*

**2. Possession by the spirit of the devil**

Jesus warned the man whom He healed of a thirty eight year old impotency:

(John 5:14)

*Afterward Jesus findeth him in the temple, and said unto him, Behold, thou art made whole: sin no more, lest a worse thing come unto thee.*

Jesus warns all men in Matthew's gospel,

(Matthew 12:43 – 45)

43 *When the unclean spirit is gone out of a man, he walketh through dry places, seeking rest, and findeth none.*

44 *Then he saith, I will return into my house from whence I came out; and when he is come, he findeth it empty, swept, and garnished.*

45 *Then goeth he, and taketh with himself seven other spirits more wicked than himself, and they enter in and dwell there: and the last state of that man is worse than the first. Even so shall it be also unto this wicked generation.*

As Jesus warned, so did James,
(James 3:13 – 18)

> 13 *Who is a wise man and endued with knowledge among you? let him shew out of a good conversation his works with meekness of wisdom.*
> 14 *But if ye have bitter envying and strife in your hearts, glory not, and lie not against the truth.*
> 15 *This wisdom descendeth not from above, but is earthly, sensual, devilish* (it is from the devil).
> 16 *For where envying and strife is, there is confusion and every evil work.*
> 17 *But the wisdom that is from above is first pure, then peaceable, gentle, and easy to be intreated, full of mercy and good fruits, without partiality, and without hypocrisy.*
> 18 *And the fruit of righteousness is sown in peace of them that make peace.*

You might think you are being wise by not forgiving; on the contrary, unknown to you, you have received "another" spirit (2 Corinthians 11:4). James is saying here that the man that is bitter and unforgiving has wisdom that is from the devil, meaning, Satan's spirit has entered into such an one.

Besides satanic wisdom (Verse 15), there is wisdom from God (Verse 17). The qualities of the wisdom from God are listed: First, it is **pure,** second, it is **peaceable;** third, it is **gentle;** fourth, it is **easy to be entreated** (that is, it can easily be begged); fifth, it is **full of mercy;** sixth, it is **full of good fruits;** seventh, it is **not partial** and eight, it is **without hypocrisy** (that is, it does not pretend).

The fruit of The Holy Spirit will not grow in you if you are the quarrelsome, fighting, unforgiving, hating person, because that fruit is sown only where there is peace and it is sown in the hearts of them that make peace.

### 3. Short Life

(1 Peter 3:10, 11)

> 10 *For he that* ***will love life, and see good days,*** *let him refrain his tongue from evil, and his lips that they speak no guile:*
>
> 11 *Let him eschew evil, and do good; let him seek peace, and ensue it.*

This is a quotation from (Psalms 34:12 – 16). He who

wishes to live long and prosperously must act as he is here directed,

i. He must refrain from evil speaking, lying and slandering.

ii. He must avoid flattery and fair speeches, which cover hypocritical or wicked intentions.

iii. He must "avoid" evil; keep "going away" from evil.

iv. He must do good; he must walk in the way of righteousness.

v. **He must live peaceably with all men; seek peace where it has been lost;** and "**pursue it" where it seems to be flying away.**

He who lives thus must live happily within himself. You do not want to die before your time? You want to live long? You want things to be better for you? **Peace! Go and make peace!**

**4. Hindered Family Prayers**

(1 Peter 3:7, 12, 13)

> 7 *Likewise, ye husbands, dwell with them according to knowledge, giving honour unto the*

*wife, as unto the weaker vessel, and as being heirs together of the grace of life; that your prayers be not hindered.*

12 *For the eyes of the Lord are over the righteous, and his ears are open unto their prayers: but the face of the Lord is against them that do evil.*

13 *And who is he that will harm you, if ye be followers of that which is good?*

God's ears will be closed to your prayers if you live in unforgiveness. Husbands and wives should learn to build together and pray together. Do not pray alone, unless there is a good reason for doing so at times. When you pray separately without your spouse because you are not on speaking or in good terms, your prayers are hindered, they are blocked. They do not reach God because His ears are closed to your prayers, and that is because you are disobeying His law of forgiveness.

*Now we know that God heareth not sinners: but if any man be a worshipper of God, and doeth his will, him he heareth.* (John 9:31)

*He that turneth away his ear from hearing the law, even his prayer shall be abomination.* (Proverbs 28:9)

**"Abomination"** is a thing that causes disgust and hatred, or is extremely offensive. If you will not hear and obey God's law, God will not hear your prayers. Actually your prayer is hateful and disgusting to God.

## 5. Rejected Offerings

God will reject your offerings or your services.
(Matthew 5:23, 24)

> 23 *Therefore if thou bring thy gift to the altar, and there rememberest that thy brother hath ought against thee.*
>
> 24 *Leave there thy gift before the altar, and go thy way: first be reconciled to thy brother, and then come and offer thy gift.*

This is as much as to say, "Do **not** attempt to bring any offering to God while you are in a spirit of enmity against any person which you have not settled". God will not accept any act of religious worship from us while any enmity subsists in our hearts towards anybody.

This is what God is saying: as you go to Church and you remember that you have a problem with somebody, leave your offering there, leave the Church (thank God these days we have mobile phones), go out, make that call and make peace with the person, after which you can return, take your offering and offer to God.

Samuel told Saul, "*...Hath the Lord as great delight in burnt offerings and sacrifices, as in obeying the voice of the Lord? Behold, to obey is better than sacrifice, and to hearken than the fat of rams.*" (1 Samuel 15:22) God is not as interested in your money as He is interested in your obedience; God is not as interested in your money as He is interested in your soul and your making Heaven; God is not as interested in your money as He is interested in your righteousness, in your living a righteous, holy life, a life that is always forgiving.

In Proverbs 21:27, we read,

> *The sacrifice of the wicked is abomination: how much more, when he bringeth it with a wicked mind?*

God is turned off by the donations of unrepentant sinners (sacrifice without righteousness). He hates it even more when a gift is intended to "buy Him off" or induce Him to condone, approve or bless some wicked scheme.

If you give that offering in disobedience, it is not to God, but to your pastor that you have given and there are many of these fake pastors who are actually looking for that money. They do not mind if you live in your hatred and unforgiving spirit so long as you give to them. Take note, such is a service to them, not to God.

**6. You will not see God, now and in eternity** (Hebrews 12:14,15)

> [14]*Follow peace with all men, and holiness, without which no man shall see the Lord:*
> [15]*Looking diligently lest any man fail of the grace of God; lest any root of bitterness springing up trouble you, and thereby many be defiled.*

Pursue after peace with all men; even when they are spoiling for trouble, run after them, and make sure you get it. Follow it through all places and circumstances *"and holiness"* – a state of continual sanctification; that life of purity and detachment from the world and all its lusts.

> *Blessed are the pure in heart: for they shall see God.* (Matthew 5:8)

A pure-hearted person is one whose thoughts are holy, whose conscience is clean.

DISTINGUISHING FACTORS BETWEEN THE CHILDREN OF GOD AND THE CHILDREN OF THE DEVIL.

> *In this the children of God are manifest, and the children of the devil:* ***whosoever*** *doeth not* ***righteousness*** *is not of God,* ***neither he that loveth not his brother.*** (1 John 3:10)

Speaking on the significance of the state of the heart Jesus taught,
(Matthew 15:18 – 20)

> 18 *But those things which proceed out of the mouth come forth from the heart; and they defile the man.* ("Defile" means "dirty", "no longer pure").
> 19 *For out of the heart proceed evil thoughts,*

*murders, adulteries, fornications, thefts, false witness, blasphemies:*
20 *These are the things which defile a man: but to eat with unwashen hands defileth not a man.*

*"These are the things which defile a man..."* In other words, you will not make heaven, which implies you will go to hell if you cannot forgive from your heart. You will not have God in your life here, you will not see His works in your life here on earth and you will not see Him in heaven hereafter because you are defiled, that is, you are dirty, you are impure.

We read of **"root of bitterness"** in Hebrews 12:15. When you plant a seed, the root will grow into the ground and it will eventually bear fruit. In like manner, "bitterness" is a root that grows in the heart and bears the fruit of unforgiveness that defiles a man, for example, a woman that refuses to forgive her husband and vice versa. **Anybody that refuses to forgive is a defiled person and a defiled person shall not enter heaven.**

*And there shall in no wise enter into it any thing*

*that defileth, neither whatsoever worketh abomination, or maketh a lie: but they which are written in the Lamb's book of life.*
(Revelation 21:27)

The disciples pleaded with Jesus, *"Increase our faith"*. I want you to pray that prayer, "God increase my faith. Give me the grace to forgive." Right where you are, forgive people. You cannot afford to miss heaven. Do as I did, call those who have offended you and forgive them because no man should make you miss heaven.

**7. God will not show mercy to you**

*Blessed are the merciful; for they shall obtain mercy.* (Matthew 5:7)

"To be merciful means to be actively compassionate. In one sense it means to withhold punishment from offenders who deserve it." (Believer's Bible Commentary – William MacDonald, 1995)

*The merciful man doeth good to his own soul: but he that is cruel troubleth his own flesh.* (Proverbs 11:17)

*With the merciful thou wilt shew thyself*

> *merciful, and with the upright man thou wilt shew thyself upright.* (2 Samuel 22:26)
> *For he shall have judgment without mercy, that hath shewed no mercy; and mercy rejoiceth against judgment.* (James 2:13)

The Living Bible translation explains James 2:13 more clearly.

> ***There will be no mercy for those who have not shown mercy to others.*** *But if you have been merciful, God will be merciful when he judges you.*

## 8. Forgive For Your Own Sake

God says in Isaiah 43:25;

> *I, even I, am he that blotteth out thy transgressions for mine own sake, and will not remember thy sins.*

What does God mean by *"for mine own sake"*? God had to forgive for His Name's sake otherwise the sacrifice of the Promised **Seed** of the woman (Jesus Christ), promised early in the threshold of human history (Genesis 3:15; Revelation 12:17), would have been in vain and His Name profaned and blasphemed amongst the fallen spirits. In like manner, if **you do not forgive** men their trespasses against you, **you will end up being at the receiving end; you end up being the one afflicted; being the one tormented; being the one suffering and being the one to be rejected by heaven at the end. When you forgive, you are forgiving for your own sake, for the sake of your spouse, your children, your business and your career, etc. Therefore, for your happiness, joy and fulfillment, for your own sake, you must forgive.**

# CHAPTER 6

# CONDITIONS FOR TOTAL FREEDOM FROM TORMENTORS (AS ITEMIZED IN CHAPTER THREE)

> *And his lord was wroth, and delivered him to the tormentors, till he should pay all that was due unto him.* (Matthew 18:34)

First, the condition for relief from tormentors is forgiveness – **"until"** you forgive. Secondly, the condition for total and complete relief from tormentors is **total forgiveness.**

THE MEASURE OR RATION OF FORGIVENESS

Luke says, *"Forgive and ye shall be forgiven".* (Luke 6:37). Matthew says, *"Forgive us our debts* ***as*** *we forgive our debtors.* (Matthew 6:12). Again Luke says, *"For with* ***the same measure*** *that ye mete withal, it shall be* ***measured unto you again"*** (Luke 6:38). Matthew also says *"With* ***what measure*** *ye mete,* ***it***

***shall be measured to you again"*** (Matthew 7:2) i.e. rationed to you.

**We** are forgiven **as we** forgive. Forgive one offense and **you** are forgiven one offense. Forgive two offenses and you are forgiven two offenses and so on and so forth. Forgiveness is progressive. It is the **few** offenses that we forgive, that we are forgiven; and it is the **much** or **many** offenses that we forgive, that we are forgiven. Mark says, *"But **if ye do not forgive, neither will your Father** which is in heaven **forgive your trespasses."*** (Mark 11:26).

Back to our illustration in Chapter Three. For each man he forgives, a tormentor leaves. When he forgives the first person, he is set free from "arthritis"; he forgives the second, "asthma" goes; he forgives the third person, "cancer" leaves, the fourth and "diabetes" goes etc.

By progressively forgiving, the man is getting freer and freer. He forgives yet another person, "skin diseases" leave. His skin becomes like a baby's. He forgives yet another person, "stomach disorder" leaves him immediately. He forgives another person, "multiple misfortunes", goes! He forgives another person – "liver disease" goes! He forgives another person – "migraine" goes! He forgives another person – "Infertility" goes! He forgives another person – "Kidney disease" goes! He forgives another person – "Mental disorder" goes! He forgives another person – "Insomnia" goes! This man is beginning to get freer and freer!

However, if he says, "God, you said I should forgive. I have forgiven so many but these remaining five people, I will not forgive them." The remaining five tormentors – fever, heart disease, hypertension, urinary disease and multiple misfortunes will also not go away, because the Lord's condition or demand is, "pay all" – forgive everybody!

The Lord's Prayer says, *"Forgive us our debts as we forgive our debtors"* (Matthew 6:12) So for the five remaining people he refuses to forgive, so also will the five attendant problems stay with him! As many or as few we forgive, as many or few we are forgiven.

But if after a while, he says "This hypertension is disturbing me too much, just because of unforgiveness? I forgive my enemy". That hypertension will now go away from him. So will the other remaining tormentors leave him as he keeps on forgiving. But if he holds back forgiveness from even one person and says "This one? I will not forgive him. Am I not a human being? Don't I have feelings? I will not forgive this man; I will not forgive that woman; I will not forgive this person or that individual for all that he or she did to me!" I want you to know beloved, neither will the last tormentor go from him/you, and it will continue to torment him/you! He and not his enemy is being tormented; you and not your enemy is being tormented; he and not his enemy is suffering; you and not your enemy is suffering. So when we forgive, it is for our own good. I forgive to live. I forgive to be free!

**Testimonies**

1. Okrika (Rivers State), Nigeria:

Okrika is an expansive riverine community in Rivers State of Nigeria consisting of a mainland and several islands. In November 1976, the Greater Evangelism World Crusade evangelical field team embarked on the second leg of the Okrika Campaign, having campaigned there earlier in 1974.

The campaign was planned to go through Ogoloma, Kalio, Abuloma and the main island of Okrika itself. But there was a problem. A communal war was imminent between the two ruling houses: "Koniju", and "Tobuniju" over which house was to produce the next Amayanabo (King).

Hitherto, there had been several clashes which had built up to this imminent major war. Both factions had demarcated their territories with tapes and concrete pillars. The State Government had sent in the mobile Police force to the territory to defuse the tension but the war cry never abated.

It was at this point in time I entered the island with my crusading team. Because of the tense atmosphere, it was not possible to set up a platform in an open area for the campaign. However, one of our very zealous sisters, by name Ada Williams, married to a military officer, offered us a two storey building complex which accommodated the team. From this point, let me quote one of the faithful elders of the Ministry and an indigene of the community – Pastor Diepiriye Jamabo:

"However, the Apostle, the visioner and the Director, directed the team to mount the speakers at the uppermost regions of the building. This directive was complied with immediately. He then asked us to eat and rest for the day. At exactly 12:00 midnight, the crusade started. The team members sang thrilling and soul refreshing songs and choruses till 2.00am. It was at this point the Apostle took up his message and it was on "Forgiveness". The crusade ended by 4.00am. The team rested and at 6.00am, the quiet time began and ended at 8.00am. This was the trend and the message the Lord directed His servant to preach for the period of the seven days the crusade lasted. There was no altar call but on daily basis, the Holy Spirit directed converts from both sides of the divide (enemy camps) in twos and threes to the camp.

The zealous young fellowship grew from strength to strength numerically and spiritually as more and more natives got interested. Then the persecutions started. The husband of the sister, the military man arrived; he was very angry with his wife for accommodating us in his house. He ordered the team together with the Apostle to get out of his house with immediate effect but he was late. The deed had been done and the task accomplished. The high point was that the crusade of our father the Apostle, put a final full stop to the sectional tribal war! The people forgave themselves!

Gradually, life became normal and all the activities, education, markets, social activities and festivals commenced till date. As at when this Holy Ghost crusade took place, the entire water front of Okrika Island was engulfed by giant mangroves. But today, they have mainly been cleared, sand-filling has taken place, a ring road built round the island and several new buildings are shooting skyward all the time. Great developments are taking place, there is progress all over **because we forgave one another and allowed**

**peace to reign.** We remain ever grateful to the Apostle and his crusading team."

2. Cotonou, Benin Republic:

There is a testimony from a Beninese lady resident in China whom I met in Cotonou, Benin Republic while teaching on "Forgiveness". Nobody prayed for her. As she heard this teaching on forgiveness, she went out to make a long distance phone call to an enemy and forgave. By the time she returned to the hall, I was praying for the congregation and "something" went out of her, she testified afterwards. That was how she was set free. Her sickness of many years left and she was made whole. Nobody prayed specially for her. Yes, it is for your own good and well-being that you forgive.

3. Parakou, Benin Republic

My name is Robert Agbogbo, I got born again in 1984 in Natitingou, North-Western part of Benin Republic. My wife, after serving voodoo in a shrine for 15 years, became a Roman Catholic and my sons: Patrick and Augustin also became Catholics. Augustin, the younger brother was helping the Reverend Fathers but later he started attending Sunday school in UEEB - Union des Églises Évangéliques du Benin (Evangelical Churches Union of Benin) Church in Agla. As for myself, for almost 30 years, I was under the power of *dangbe* (python spirit) that would come to my house every month wherever I lived with my family. I gave my life to Christ and all the curses associated with that satanic power were broken.

On 24th March 1991, a tribal war broke out in Parakou, Benin Republic in which many people were killed. My family was scattered for about a month before we came back together again.

Early in 2004, a false prophet from Ivory Coast came to Parakou and took over the new house fellowship that my son Augustin, started with some friends before traveling with his wife to Port Harcourt to join the Greater Evangelism World Crusade (GEWC) Ministry. This false prophet destroyed the work with false prophecies, heresies and divination. At a point, he told my son, Patrick that I was the source of the problems in his life. Soon after, he cut off ignorantly from us and his brother when he received another false prophecy that said I had blessed his younger brother (Augustin) but had cursed him. This development scattered the family even worse than during the war. It was so bad that there was no more communication between him and the rest of the family. So he left Parakou and relocated first to Burkina Faso, then to northern Togo and in 2007 he came back but stayed in Natitingou, another city in Benin Republic.

My son Pastor Augustin had earlier told me how he met Apostle Numbere on the MV DOULOS ship. By the time he left with his wife Rebecca for training in GEWC Bible College in Nigeria, the Lord spoke clearly to me that he had finally found the right way. I encouraged them to go without fear and hoped that they would come back to establish the Ministry in Benin.

Few months later by the leading of the Holy Spirit, as an elder in the church, I had a meeting with my pastor with whom I had stayed for 17 years to tender my resignation after which I started a house fellowship early 2005 under a mango tree for Greater Evangelism World Crusade. By faith, just by hearing testimonies that my son Augustin and his wife were sharing with me on phone without even knowing the doctrine and the leader of the ministry, I was strongly moved by the Spirit of God that it is a genuine ministry and a source of hope once more for my family. There is now a strong work in Parakou and a base for the northern work of GEWC in Benin Republic. To God be the glory.

In March 2008 (5th-9th) the International Director, his wife and his team came to Parakou for their first visit. I was personally so excited because while leading the prayer band for this visit, I had a ministration to invite my estranged son Patrick to this program, that Apostle Numbere's visit would bring about the total deliverance of my family. By this time, he had cut off from us for about four years but I believed the Lord and invited him anyway.

The first miracle was that he agreed to come. The teaching was the second miracle. This was the first time since I gave my life to Christ I had ever heard this type of teaching about "Forgiveness" . The teaching was so practical and it was followed by testimonies every day. I still remember the illustration about the consequences of unforgiveness – sickness, destruction etc.

I couldn't help crying almost every day during the duration of the program and I could tell my son Patrick was also feeling the same way during the meetings. On Saturday before the service commenced, I and my wife called our sons for a meeting around 5 a.m. This gathering quickly became very emotional as we forgave one another and all of us prayed together as a family.

For my wife Mary Agbogbo and me, it was like a New Year resolution. Since that time, we have been so blessed: I am alive to see my two sons become full time ministers in the same ministry; I am totally healed and getting stronger every year with my wife; many times the Lord delivered me from death, and many other blessings. When I visited the World Headquarters for the 40th anniversary of the Ministry,

I became certain that I did not miss my way. I sincerely want to thank God Almighty, the International Director, and his wife for their love and I want to use this opportunity to tell anyone reading this testimony that there is power in forgiveness, I am a living testimony of this.

4. Liberia:

In 2009, I went for a mission in Liberia. It was a country that had been torn by two civil wars over a period of fourteen years. A lot of atrocities had been committed by the different warring factions. Many individuals and families had been scarred permanently with resultant bitterness, hatred and deep desire for revenge against their enemies. It was against this background that I taught on "Forgiveness". The effect of the teaching was dramatic as illustrated by these two testimonies.

- My name is Daniel B. Kollie and I am from Liberia. During the Liberian civil war in 2003, Mr. Daniel Chea, the Minister of Defense during the regime of former President Charles Taylor, announced on KISS FM (a local radio station), that the

Gbandi tribe was supporting Liberians United for Reconciliation and Democracy (LURD), one of the warring factions in the Liberia civil war.

Tribal differences, marginalization of the under privileged and corruption at the highest level were all factors that were deeply rooted in the Liberian civil crisis. The nation was so terrible to the extent that the life of a cock was being valued more than the lives of human beings. Guns were in the hands of little boys who were under the influences of drugs and demonic powers to kill anyone they desired. Therefore, such a statement coming from the Defense Minister at that time brought the lives of many innocent people under threat including my family who were residing in Mowulahun Town, Lofa County. Over hundred persons were slaughtered in my village between Kabolahun and Mowulahun by General Blama and his boys who were under direct instructions of the Defense Minister to kill the Gbandi people. My elder Sister (Damawa Hally) was killed with her two children, (Kumba

Hally and Kpehe Hally). Worst of all, my sister Damawa Hally was nine months pregnant when she was killed. My little sister Mamie was also brutally raped by the same people who killed my elder sister. All these happened because Mr. Daniel Chea had labeled my innocent family as supporters of the so called LURD (a rebel group). After this incidence befell my family, I developed deep hatred for Mr. Daniel Chea. I planned to avenge the death of my loved ones even if it cost my life. I became a secret enemy of this man for many years. In fact on one occasion, out of several others, I attempted breaking a bottle on his head at the Vamoma service station but was prevented by a waitress.

To the glory of God, all this came to an end when the International Director of Greater Evangelism World Crusade (GEWC), Apostle G. D. Numbere visited Liberia in 2009. I was privileged to be part of the "Caught Up" Crusade held on the airfield, opposite the Fish Market. In one of the morning teaching sessions at the Base Church of GEWC,

Sinkor, Liberia, Apostle G. D. Numbere taught on "Forgiveness". His teaching that day transformed my entire perception about life. From his teaching I discovered that an unforgiving spirit would lead us to hell and also bring about several sicknesses in our lives.

He demonstrated on the sheets of paper the kinds of torment and imprisonment we invite into our lives when we fail to forgive those who have hurt us. This was the first obvious teaching on forgiveness I had ever heard and seen in my life. With tears in my eyes, I stood up in that meeting and shared my experience. The tears that gushed out of my eyes took away the burden from my heart that the "ten million dollar" worth Truth and Reconciliation Commission (TRC) set up by the Government to reconcile the Liberian people could not do. Jesus did it for me through the teaching of His Servant and my spiritual life has changed. I am free from the torment of an unforgiving spirit and can boldly say I am a child of God. Today I am in a

Church where the truth is being taught and the blessings of God flow. Thank God for Daddy (Apostle G. D. Numbere), Pastor Manga, Evangelist Joshua Wright Samura and Greater Evangelism World Crusade family for their commitment to the Ministry in Liberia.

- Another man in that same situation as Daniel Kollie also finally decided to forgive his enemy, even though it was difficult for him to do so, and immediately his heart disease left. He was cured without a single prayer being said for him. Just by forgiving, he was set free and he became a free man.

5. Ponte Noire, Congo Brazzaville

In September 2012, I went for a mission to the Republic of Congo commonly referred to as Congo Brazzaville. In my message, I taught on forgiveness, using the illustration of tormentors that could come on someone who did not forgive. The people understood and obeyed the Word. The next day I called for testimonies. People came out to give testimonies of healings and deliverances they received when they forgave those who offended them. As they forgave, their blindness, deafness, heart diseases, etc. were healed with no prayers said! Pastors were busy the whole day reconciling with one another and more people gave their lives to Christ.

Sample Testimonies

- A young man, a pastor, had been suffering from urinary tract infection for sixteen years and heart disease for ten years. During my message on forgiveness, he realized that his ailments started when he refused to forgive those who had offended him, one of whom was a fellow pastor and all those years he harboured ill feelings against them. He decided to forgive all of them, and called them and made peace. He was healed instantly.
- A young lady, also a pastor, had for many years deep bitterness against those who had mistreated or offended her. She had been sick for a long time, afflicted with many diseases which meant frequent visits to the hospital. A

doctor had even diagnosed her to be suffering from eleven diseases. She was touched by the message on forgiveness. She went home and forgave, reconciled with all her enemies and was healed of all her diseases. She asked the doctor to write down all those diseases on a paper for her. She came and presented the paper for all to see as she testified.

- A young lady was suffering from impaired hearing in her right ear for a long time. She had been to hospital for treatment but instead of her condition improving, it became worse. A friend of hers heard and prevailed on her to attend the Conference. She testified that she had never heard such a teaching before, that unforgiveness could cause afflictions in a person. She had a long standing enmity with her brother to the point that when he was getting married, she had refused to be involved in his wedding. She was convicted by the message. Immediately after the meeting she called her brother and reconciled with him. She was healed that same day.

- An ordained elder in one of the churches had problems with his pastor and the pastor's wife. He was so hurt and angry that he left the church and for more than one year, he kept away from church. Incidentally, the Pastor and his wife were in the Conference. The man received the word of God, obeyed and went and made peace with them right there in the hall. They hugged themselves as they forgave one another and were all filled with overwhelming joy.
- Another young man who had been keeping malice with his aunty and her children called her right after the talk. He promised to call her later in the night after the programme. Somehow he was unable to make the call after we dismissed that night, so very early the next morning, he called her and reconciled with her. He obtained the telephone numbers of her children from her and called them one after the other and made peace with all of them.

**Leaving Vengeance to God – A Few Testimonies**

1. Kigali, Rwanda:

In the year 2000, I went on a mission to Kigali,

Rwanda's capital. At that time, the Rwandans were just coming out of war and their condition was pitiable. The ethnic war and ethnic cleansing that took place among the Hutus and Tutsis is common knowledge. The killings were so terrible that whole families were completely wiped out and many children became orphans. Even among the survivors, there was hardly any family that was complete. As a result of the destruction and killings, there was so much mistrust, bitterness and hatred for one another among the people. There was much anger and pain stuffed in their hearts towards one another – the Hutus against the Tutsis and vice versa. So much was the bitterness that nobody preached forgiveness. I did not know about this but I was led by the Lord to preach on forgiveness. God so brought the teaching to bear on the people that at a point they were just weeping. You know when you are very bitter in your spirit, when someone tells you to forgive, it is always a struggle. I pressed on with my message, and they wept as they battled in their hearts.

One night after I had ministered, a lady came to see

me. She told me of the great struggle she had had in her heart after hearing my sermon on forgiveness. She began, "I have sat through your teaching on forgiveness. I was touched, but I do not know what forgiveness is. I want to forgive but I can't. Please tell me what to do because I do not know what I can do to forgive. For you to understand why I can't, let me first tell you my story." She then told me her story. She said that during that period of ethnic crisis, her husband and her children were killed in her presence and then she was violently gang raped. She had no idea how many men raped her for they were so many. They raped her until her waist broke and she died, and even after she died they were still raping her corpse. She did not know how she came back to life but she had contacted HIV/AIDS from those who raped her. The United Nations health workers did all they could for her and took her to a number of hospitals but she lost her uterus (womb). She said, "Look at me, I am an HIV/AIDS patient. I do not know how many more days I have to live. Your message on forgiveness, I like it and I understand. I want to forgive but tell me, what is forgiveness?" she was crying as she told her story. I too wept along with her. Such a beautiful young lady, and for such a life to be so wasted?

She continued, "Inside of me, I appreciate what you preached, but how do I go about it? I do not know what forgiveness is because every day that I wake up and find myself alive, I have things in my body telling me, 'somebody did this to you!' I do not even know those men, but I hate everybody." She sobbed, "I hate everybody, I do not want to hear the name of tribes. I just hate everybody!"

I could not speak for a while. In my mind I asked God for wisdom. "Lord, please give me a word for this lady," I prayed. Finally, the Lord gave me a word for her. Speaking gently, I said, "Sister, I understand your state of mind. I understand, but look, the Lord said, '*Vengeance is mine, I will repay*'. Even if all those men that did this to you were around, you are but a weak young lady, can you fight any of them? They have destroyed everything that mattered in your life. They have dislocated your system. They have given you a sickness that is incurable. Yes, on this side of life, they have damaged you irreparably. Human beings have made you lose out on this side of life. Would you also allow human beings to make you lose out on heaven? The Lord said if you do not forgive them that you would not be forgiven. It means you will also lose heaven. Would you like to lose on both sides? Why would you lose here and also lose heaven? Do not allow man to make you lose heaven. I know you are a human being. I feel like you do. Who would not feel the way you feel? But this is the very thing you must not allow to make you lose heaven. Since the Lord has said, ***'Vengeance is mine, I will repay',*** leave the vengeance to Him. If only you can say, 'Lord, I leave everything in your Hands; I forgive all those people', God's grace will heal these festering wounds in your hearts. And after what other days you have to live here on earth, you will go into the presence of Jesus Christ where you will know no more pain. All of these things will not be there in heaven. You will not have HIV/AIDS in heaven; you will not be missing your uterus in heaven; you will not have a broken waist in heaven. There will be no damage to your life and to your body. Jesus will take care of all that. You will be free!"

She started crying again and I started crying with her again. As I ministered, the Holy Spirit came in and removed her burden. She heaved a sigh of relief, brightened up as a small smile broke out on her lips and crept across her face.

"Thank you Pastor", she told me. "This is what I needed to hear. I will obey. Now I forgive them whoever they are".

2. Okrika (Rivers State), Nigeria

In 1980, Late Chief Melford Okilo's government made a massive reclamation of the mangroves in most of the water fronts in the State. Okrika was a beneficiary and the whole of the present ring road area was reclaimed. The reclaimed lands were given a space of time to settle down. The brethren of the Ministry did all within their reach to secure a piece of land on this reclaimed land for their church building but the community would not allow them. This resulted in a protracted land case between the Church and the community which came to an end due to repeated deaths of those who were spearheading the case from the families, particularly that of Odo-Abaji and Kalipa. In the year 1984, the Port Harcourt brethren from Okrika tasked themselves to build a wooden structure on the land allocated to them on the sand-filled area for worship. As at then, the Church also had few challenges that emanated from the Odo-Abaji war canoe house (with the reason that the said parcel of land allocated to the Church was on their old settlement). By the time we came back the next morning, the wooden structure had been completely destroyed by them. They also threatened us to vacate the place or else they would shoot us from a distance.

One particular man from that family boasted that he would not live to see the Church develop that property. He boasted that he would shoot anyone doing so except he had gone blind. According to his statement, one mid-day, he paraded to see if truly the rumour of our development was correct. On confirmation, he managed to reach his house with the intention of picking his gun and return to make good his threat. But his eyes were struck blind by the angels of the Lord. He remained blind for the rest of his days on earth. **Vengeance belongs to God!**

(Deuteronomy 32:35a)

*To me belongeth vengeance, and recompence;*

(Psalms 94:1)

*O Lord God, to whom vengeance belongeth; O God, to whom vengeance belongeth, shew thyself.*

(Psalms 18:47)

*It is God that avengeth me, and subdueth the people under me.*

(Romans 12:19-21)

[19]*Dearly beloved, avenge not yourselves, but rather give place unto wrath: for it is written, Vengeance is mine; I will repay, saith the Lord.*

[20] *Therefore if thine enemy hunger, feed him; if he thirst, give him drink: for in so doing thou shalt heap coals of fire on his head.*

[21] *Be not overcome of evil, but overcome evil with good.*

(Hebrews 10:30)

*For we know him that hath said, Vengeance belongeth unto me, I will recompense, saith the Lord. And again, The Lord shall judge his people.*

# CHAPTER 7

# PRE-LAW VENGEANCE

**Vengeance preceded the Law**

Cain had murdered his younger brother Abel out of jealousy.

(Genesis 4:2 – 8)

> 2 *And she again bare his brother Abel. And Abel was a keeper of sheep, but Cain was a tiller of the ground.*
>
> 3 *And in process of time it came to pass, that Cain brought of the fruit of the ground an offering unto the Lord.*
>
> 4 *And Abel, he also brought of the firstlings of his flock and of the fat thereof. And the Lord had respect unto Abel and to his offering:*
>
> 5 *But unto Cain and to his offering he had not respect. And Cain was very wroth, and his countenance fell.*
>
> 6 *And the Lord said unto Cain, Why art thou wroth? And why is thy countenance fallen?*

> [7] *If thou doest well, shalt thou not be accepted? And if thou doest not well, sin lieth at the door. And unto thee shall be his desire, and thou shalt rule over him.*
>
> [8] *And Cain talked with Abel his brother: and it came to pass, when they were in the field, that Cain rose up against Abel his brother, and slew him."*

Based on this murder, Abel's blood cried unto the Lord for vengeance.

> *And he said* (to Cain), *what hast thou done?* ***the voice of thy brother's blood crieth unto me from the ground.*** (Genesis 4:10)

Following this, God took vengeance on Cain.

THE VENGEANCE OR JUDGMENTS ON CAIN (Genesis 4:11 – 12)

> [11] *And now art thou cursed from the earth, which hath opened her mouth to receive thy brother's blood from thy hand;*
>
> [12] *When thou tillest the ground, it shall not henceforth yield unto thee her strength; a fugitive and a vagabond shalt thou be in the earth.*

1. Cain was cursed.
2. His farmland was cursed.
3. He would be a fugitive and a vagabond.

Following this, Cain was alarmed and appealed to God for mitigation of his punishment.

CAIN'S ANALYSIS OF GOD'S JUDGMENT ON HIM (Genesis 4:13 – 14)

> 13 *And Cain said unto the Lord, My punishment is greater than I can bear.*
>
> 14 *Behold, thou hast driven me out this day from the face of the earth; and from thy face shall I be hid; and I shall be a fugitive and a vagabond in the earth; and it shall come to pass, that every one that findeth me shall slay me.*

1. He would be driven out from, eliminated from the earth.
2. He would not see God's face, meaning, God would hide His face from Cain.
3. He would be a fugitive and a vagabond.

On the basis of his appeal, God said to Cain:

## 1. Sevenfold Vengeance

(Genesis 4:15)

> *And the Lord said unto him, therefore* ***whosoever slayeth Cain, vengeance shall be taken on him sevenfold.*** *And the Lord set a mark upon Cain, lest any finding him should kill him.*
>
> *The Lord replied, "They won't kill you, for* ***I will give seven times your punishment to anyone who does."*** (Living Bible).

This was what David was reminding God in Psalms 79:12 – 13

> 12 *And* ***render unto our neighbours sevenfold into their bosom their reproach,*** *wherewith they have reproached thee, O Lord.*
>
> 13 *So we thy people and sheep of thy pasture will give thee thanks for ever: we will shew forth thy praise to all generations.*

## 2. Seventy And Sevenfold Vengeance

THE GENERATION OF CAIN was noted for murder.

CAIN (Genesis 4:8) — **1st Murder** in the History of Mankind

↓

ENOCH (Genesis 4:17)

↓

IRAD (Genesis 4:18)

↓

MEHUJAEL (Genesis 4:18)

↓

METHUSAEL (Genesis 4:18)

↓

LAMECH (Genesis 4:23) — **2nd Murder** in the History of Mankind

Many years after Cain, his fifth generation son, Lamech (Genesis 4:17 – 18) confessed to his wives that he also, like his great, great, great grandfather Cain, had slain a man (committed murder).

> *And Lamech said unto his wives, Adah and Zillah, Hear my voice; ye wives of Lamech, hearken unto my speech: for I have slain a man*

> *to my wounding, and a young man to my hurt.* (Genesis 4:23)

There was "murder" in Cain's blood-line!

At this, Lamech recalled the vengeance taken on Cain, his great, great, great grandfather and said to his wives,

> *If Cain shall be* ***avenged sevenfold,*** *truly Lamech* ***seventy and sevenfold.*** (Genesis 4:24)

# CHAPTER 8

# AMENDMENT OF LAWS

| | |
|---|---|
| **PRE-LAW** | **SEVENTY AND SEVEN FOLD VENGEANCE**<br>• *If **Cain** shall be **avenged sevenfold,** truly **Lamech seventy and sevenfold**.* (Genesis 4:24) |
| **OLD TESTAMENT LAW** | **TIT FOR TAT (EQUALITY OF VENGEANCE)**<br>• *Breach for breach, eye for eye, tooth for tooth: as he hath caused a blemish in a man, so shall it be done to him again.* (Leviticus 24:20) |
| **JESUS CHRIST (GRACE)** | **FORGIVENESS AND LOVE**<br>• *And when ye stand praying, forgive, if ye have ought against any: that your Father also which is in heaven may forgive you your trespasses. But if ye do not forgive, neither will your Father which is in heaven forgive your trespasses.* (Mark 11:25-26) |

AMENDMENT OF PRE-LAW VENGEANCE BY THE OLD TESTAMENT LAW

The Old Testament law amended or mitigated the Pre-law vengeance of "SEVENTY FOLD" to "TIT FOR TAT." In the LAW, men were not allowed to exact more penalty than was due. They were limited to "equality of vengeance".

**Tit For Tat, an Eye for an Eye**

(Leviticus 24:17 – 22)

> 17 *And* ***he that killeth any man shall surely be put to death.***
>
> 18 *And he that killeth a beast shall make it good;* ***beast for beast.***
>
> 19 *And if a man cause a blemish in his neighbour;* ***as he hath done, so shall it be done to him;***
>
> 20 ***Breach for breach, eye for eye, tooth for tooth: as he hath caused a blemish in a man, so shall it be done to him again.***
>
> 21 ***And he that killeth a beast, he shall restore it: and he that killeth a man, he shall be put to death.***
>
> 22 *Ye shall have one manner of law, as well for the*

*stranger, as for one of your own country: for I am the Lord your God.*

**Witches and Wizards Not To Be Allowed To Live**

*Thou shalt not suffer a witch to live.*

(Exodus 22:18)

It has been pointed out in those passages that we have a limitation to the right of retaliation – not more than an eye for an eye, a tooth for a tooth. What is intended and permitted here is no more than "full and just indemnity".

AMENDMENT OR MITIGATION OF THE OLD TESTAMENT LAW BY JESUS CHRIST

In the New Testament Jesus amended or mitigated the Old Testament law of "TIT FOR TAT" to "FORGIVENESS" and "LOVE".

**How Jesus Addressed Specific Issues**

In Matthew 5, beginning from Verse 27, Jesus addressed specific issues and topics. He addressed,

1. Adultery (Matthew 5:27 – 28)
2. Divorce (Matthew 5:21 – 32)

3. Taking of Oaths (Matthew 5:33 – 37)
4. "Tit for tat" or retaliation (Matthew 5:38 – 39)

**"Tit For Tat" Or "Retaliation" Amended**
(Matthew 5:38 – 39)

> 38 *Ye have heard that it hath been said, An eye for an eye, and a tooth for a tooth:*
> 39 ***But I say unto you, That ye resist not evil: but whosoever shall smite thee on thy right cheek, turn to him the other also.***

Thus Jesus renounced **"Tit for Tat" or "Retaliation"** and replaced it with **"Forgiveness"** and **"Love".**

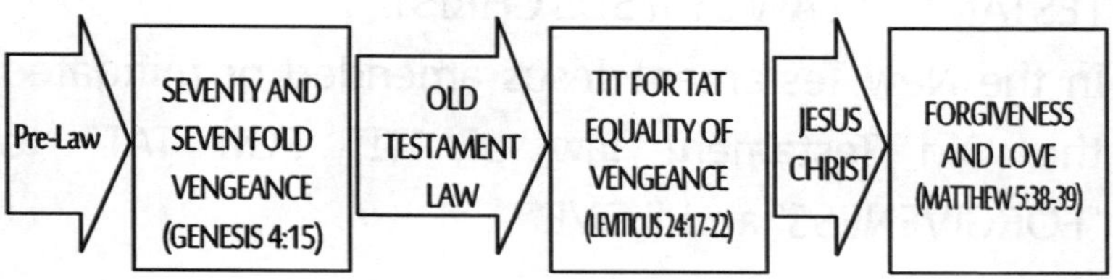

LOVE YOUR ENEMIES

In the following nine Verses of St. Luke's gospel, Jesus teaches in depth on what our attitude should be towards our enemies.

(Luke 6:27 – 36)

27 *But I say unto* ***you which hear, Love your enemies, do good to them which hate you,***

28 ***Bless*** *them that curse you, and* ***pray*** *for them which despitefully use you.*

29 *And unto him* ***that smiteth thee on the one cheek offer also the other;*** *and him that taketh away thy cloke forbid not to take thy coat also.*

30 *Give to every man that asketh of thee; and of him that taketh away thy goods ask them not again.*

31 ***And as ye would that men should do to you, do ye also to them likewise.***

32 *For if ye love them which love you, what thank have ye? for sinners also love those that love them.*

33 *And if ye do good to them which do good to you, what thank have ye? for sinners also do*

*even the same.*

*[34]And if ye lend to them of whom ye hope to receive, what thank have ye? for sinners also lend to sinners, to receive as much again.*

*[35]But **love ye your enemies, and do good,** and lend, hoping for nothing again; **and your reward shall be great, and ye shall be the children of the Highest: for he is kind unto the unthankful and to the evil.***

*[36]**Be ye therefore merciful,** as your Father also is merciful.*

In his letter to the brethren Peter wrote:

(1 Peter 3:8 – 9)

*[8]Finally, be ye all of one mind, having compassion one of another, love as brethren, be pitiful, be courteous:*

*[9]Not rendering evil for evil, or railing for railing: but contrariwise blessing; knowing that ye are thereunto called, that ye should inherit a blessing.*

## A LIVING EXAMPLE

There was a chief in the village of Yeghe in Ogoniland, Rivers State, Nigeria. In 1980, towards the end of the year, his first daughter was to get married. After the wedding in the Church, everyone moved to the venue for the reception.

There developed an impasse at the reception. The father of the bride, Chief Mato, wanted to serve alcoholic drinks but the Christians would not allow him. It was a very difficult situation in which no progress could be made because the two parties involved could not agree, could not come to terms; there was a stalemate.

It was at this juncture I arrived at the venue (rushing in from an overnight journey) and both parties – the Christians and some friends of Chief Mato approached me to proffer a solution. After debriefing both sides, I asked to see Chief Mato, whereupon I was escorted to meet him in one of the ante-rooms. On getting there, he was bent down arranging his alcoholic drinks in cartons and his attention was called to listen to an arbiter. He was too upset to even look up and see the "arbiter", not to talk of listening to him. I was asked by one of the chiefs to introduce myself. I did. It was on hearing the name "Apostle G. D. Numbere" that Chief Mato paid attention. He looked up fiendishly at me and in a rage of anger and fury rushed at me and jumping up, he gave me a very dirty slap on my right cheek – before everyone standing by! SHOCK! Sparks flew out of my eyes and my sun shade spectacle flew off my face! Meantime he continued cursing and raving at me, "Apostle Numbere, wicked man. You broke and divided my family. Go and call the police!"

I replied "God bless you. There is no need calling the police, you are already under arrest". Meanwhile, he continued raving, abusing and cursing me and daring me to call the police. Chief Mato and I had not met each other face to face before but I had heard stories of his bitterness toward me for leading his children and his estranged wife to the Lord!

I quietly moved out of the room to the long verandah.

I was yet discussing what had just happened with a brother from my Ministry (Elder Sam Ekpo) when Chief Mato surfaced again. I had thought he was passing by but he suddenly turned towards me and gave a second dirty slap, this time on the left cheek! He continued raving, cursing and abusing me for "scattering his family" because I had led them to Christ. "Go and call the police, you wicked man!" he urged. On my part, I continued to say, "God bless you. No need calling the police because you are already under arrest". I was calm, cool and collected as this whole scene played out in full glare of the public, before all the marriage guests. I never retaliated neither did I curse back.

Meantime, his fellow chiefs and friends felt so let down and disappointed, they grabbed him, bundled him into his car and drove him away. Now the wedding reception could go on without serving alcoholic drinks! Matthew 5:39 was practically fulfilled in my life that day! I turned the other cheek to be slapped! The whole assembly, including the newlywed couple (though thoroughly embarrassed) glorified

God, saying, "We have never seen it in this fashion before".

How did Mato fare afterward? In the second year after this incident, his provisions store went up in flames. As a retired civil servant, this shop was his source of livelihood. Out of shock, his right hand (the one he used in slapping me) got paralyzed followed by total body paralysis. Exactly **two years** thereafter, he passed on – he died. That man gave me **two** slaps and lived only **two** years thereafter! **I did not curse him, rather I blessed him.** In doing so, I was obeying the injunctions of Luke 6:28, ***"Bless them that curse you*** *and* ***pray for them which despitefully use you",*** and Matthew 5:39 *"But I say unto you,* ***that ye resist not evil: but whosoever shall smite thee on the right cheek, turn to him the other also",*** as well as Romans 12:19, *"Dearly beloved,* ***avenge not yourselves, but rather give place unto wrath: for it is written, vengeance is mine; I will repay, saith the Lord".*** What we suffer for His sake should be left to Him to reprove or punish. The insult is offered to Him, not to us.

## JESUS CONDEMNATION OF "TIT FOR TAT" OR RETALIATION

In the following passages, Jesus gives a barrage of teachings to condemn "Retaliation" or "Tit for Tat" or "Destruction of lives" by whatever means including prayers.

1. **Jesus' Question To The Scribes And Pharisees**

   *Then said Jesus unto them, I will ask you one thing;* ***Is it lawful on the Sabbath days to do good, or to do evil? to save life, or to destroy it?*** (Luke 6:9)

2. **Jesus' Reply To The Pharisees Query As To Why He Ate With Publicans And Sinners**

   (Matthew 9:12 – 13)

   12 *But when Jesus heard that, he said unto them, They that be whole need not a physician, but they that are sick.*

   13 *But go ye and learn what that meaneth,* ***I will have mercy, and not sacrifice****: for I am not come to call the righteous, but sinners to repentance.*

3. **Jesus Rebuking His Disciples For Wanting To Take Vengeance**

   *For the Son of man is not come to destroy men's lives, but to save them...* (Luke 9:56)

4. **Jesus To Zacchaeus, A Chief Among The Publicans**

   *For the Son of man is come to seek and to save that which was lost.* (Luke 19:10)

5. **Jesus' Teaching To Nicodemus, The Pharisee**

   *For God sent not his Son into the world to condemn the world; but that the world through him might be saved.* (John 3:17)

6. **Jesus' Teaching To The Jews**

   *The thief cometh not,* ***but for to steal, and to kill, and to destroy: I am come that they might have life, and that they might have it more abundantly.*** (John 10:10)

7. **Paul To Timothy On The Mission Of Jesus**

   *This is a faithful saying, and worthy of all*

*acceptation, that Christ Jesus came into the world* ***to save sinners****; of whom I am chief.* (1Timothy 1:15)

**8. Peter To The Church**

*The Lord is... longsuffering to us-ward,* ***not willing that any should perish, but that all should come to repentance.*** (2 Peter 3:9b)

# CHAPTER 9

# FORGIVENESS IN THE CHURCH

VENGEFUL SPIRIT: THE UNFORGIVING DISCIPLES

Believers and followers of Jesus Christ could be violent and unforgiving sometimes. This truth is borne out in an incident that took place between the disciples of Jesus Christ and the people of a Samaritan village.

(Luke 9:51 – 56)

> 51 *And it came to pass, when the time was come that he should be received up, he stedfastly set his face to go to Jerusalem,*
>
> 52 *And sent messengers before his face: and they went, and entered into a village of the Samaritans, to make ready for him.*
>
> 53 ***And they did not receive him**, because his face was as though he would go to Jerusalem.*
>
> 54 *And when **his disciples James and John** saw this, they said, **Lord, wilt thou that we command fire to come down from heaven,***

***and consume them, even as Elias did?***
55 ***But he turned, and rebuked them, and said, Ye know not what manner of spirit ye are of.***
56 ***For the Son of man is not come to destroy men's lives, but to save them****. And they went to another village.* (Compare Luke 19:10) *"For the Son of man is come to seek and to save that which was lost."*

**The Incident**

Jesus was to pass through this village of Samaria to go to Jerusalem (Verses 51, 52). The villagers denied Him the right of passage through their village (Verse 53). Two of His disciples, James and John were infuriated by this (Verse 54).

They made a request of Jesus to allow them ***"Command fire to come down from heaven, and consume them, even as Elias did?"*** (Verse 54)

**Jesus' Reply to James and John**

*But* ***he turned, and rebuked them,*** *and said,* ***Ye know not what manner of spirit ye are of.*** (Verse 55)

First, **"He turned".** Jesus was taken aback and shocked that His own disciples should make such a request. Secondly, **"He rebuked them".** To "rebuke" is to "reprimand". To "reprimand" is "to tell officially that you do not approve of an action or a request". Jesus rebuked and reprimanded James and John. He did not stop at that, He went on to indict them *"Ye know not what manner of spirit ye are of"*.

LESSONS TO BE LEARNED FROM JESUS' REBUKE

**Lesson 1: Having "The Spirit of God"**

The Bible teaches that if any one does not have the Spirit of Christ, he is none of His, he is not a Christian and he does not belong to God.

> *But ye are not in the flesh, but in the Spirit, if so be that the Spirit of God dwell in you.* ***Now if any man have not the Spirit of Christ, he is none of his.*** (Romans 8:9)

His disciples were believers and all of them had the Holy Spirit dwelling in them. So when in Luke 9:55 Jesus turned and rebuked His disciples, James and John, saying, *"Ye know not what manner of spirit ye are of"*, He was saying to them, "What is in you is the Holy

Spirit of God and not the spirit of the devil. It is the devil that always seeks to revenge, to avenge and to kill."

We are therefore warned,

> *Be sober, be vigilant; because your adversary the devil, as a roaring lion, walketh about, seeking whom he may devour:* (1 Peter 5:8)

The devil is a killer!

Addressing the Jews on one occasion, Jesus said to them,

> *Ye are of your father the devil, and the lusts of your father ye will do. He was a murderer from the beginning, and abode not in the truth, because there is no truth in him. When he speaketh a lie, he speaketh of his own: for he is a liar, and the father of it.* (John 8:44)

The devil is a murderer.

- **The Spirit Of God**

But we Christians are of God and have in us the Spirit of God; because of this,

i. We are to live in the Spirit
*If we live in the Spirit...* (Galatians 5:25)

ii. We are to walk in the Spirit
*...Let us also walk in the Spirit.* (Galatians 5:25) and

iii. We are to be led by the Spirit
*But if ye be led of the Spirit...* (Galatians 5:18)

- **The Spirit Of Christ**

We also have the Spirit of Christ. The Spirit of Christ is amongst other qualities,

i. The Spirit of FORGIVING
*Then said Jesus, Father, forgive them; for they know not what they do...* (Luke 23:34)

ii. The Spirit of MERCY
*For I desired mercy, and not sacrifice...* (Hosea 6:6). God puts compassion before service.

iii. The Spirit of LOVE
*And walk in love, as Christ also hath loved us, and hath given himself for us an offering and a sacrifice to God for a sweet smelling savour.* (Ephesians 5:2)

iv. The Spirit of MEEKNESS and GENTLENESS

*Take my yoke upon you, and learn of me; for I am meek and lowly in heart: and ye shall find rest unto your souls.* (Matthew 11:29)

*Now I Paul myself beseech you by the meekness and gentleness of Christ, who in presence am base among you, but being absent am bold toward you:* (2 Corinthians 10:1)

*I am sending you out as sheep among wolves. Be as wary as serpents and* ***harmless as doves****.* (Matthew 10:16 – The Living Bible)

Be mild and meek; be wise NOT to hurt; use the harmlessness of the dove to bear injuries. The Spirit descended on Christ as a dove, and all believers partake of the Spirit of Christ, a dove-like spirit made for love and peace, not for war.

v. The Spirit of LONG-SUFFERING

*Or despisest thou the riches of his goodness and forbearance and longsuffering; not knowing that the goodness of God leadeth thee to repentance?* (Romans 2:4)

vi. The Spirit of COMPASSION

***But he, being full of compassion, forgave their iniquity, and destroyed them not: yea, many a time turned he his anger away, and did not stir up all his wrath.*** (Psalms 78:38)

vii. The Spirit of SALVATION

*Who is this that cometh from Edom, with dyed garments from Bozrah? This that is glorious in his apparel, travelling in the greatness of his strength? I that speak in righteousness, mighty to save.* (Isaiah 63:1)

viii. The Spirit of LIBERATION

*The Spirit of the Lord God is upon me; because the Lord hath anointed me to preach good tidings unto the meek; he hath sent me to bind up the brokenhearted, to proclaim liberty to the captives, and the opening of the prison to them that are bound;* (Isaiah 61:1)

ix. The Spirit of TENDERNESS

*He shall feed his flock like a shepherd: He shall*

*gather the lambs with his arm, and carry them in his bosom, and shall **gently** lead those that are with young.* (Isaiah 40:11)

**Lesson 2: Power and Its Application**

James and John by this request to call down fire from heaven to consume the Samaritans, showed a great confidence and pride in the power they had received from Jesus Christ. Jesus had empowered them and commissioned them:

> *And heal the sick that are therein, and say unto them, The kingdom of God is come nigh unto you.* (Luke 10:9)

So they wished to invoke a punitive miracle upon the villagers using as an excuse the Old Testament precedent of what Elijah did (2 Kings 1:9 – 16). But Jesus knew that that outward show of loyalty and love for Him came out of a vain, showy and proud spirit! They wanted to show off the power they had received. How ready are men to misapply the examples of good men!

**Lesson 3: Saving and Not Destroying Lives**

Jesus promptly rebuked them saying, ***"...The Son of man is not come to destroy men's lives, but to save them..."*** (Luke 9:56).

i. He had not come to destroy men's lives but to save them!

ii. This was the acceptable year of the Lord. In Isaiah 61:2, there is the three-fold prophecy about His (Jesus) mission,
   a. "To proclaim the acceptable year of the Lord",
   b. "The days of vengeance of our God",
   c. "To comfort all that mourn".

When He came into Nazareth, in the temple, He was given the Bible to read. He opened to Luke 4 and read Verses 18 to 19 only. Now Verses 18 to 19 are the equivalent Verses of Isaiah 61:1–2. Isaiah 61:2 specifically reads *"To proclaim the acceptable year of the Lord, and the day of vengeance of our God..."*

When He read, He stopped His reading on the first line, *"To proclaim the acceptable year of the Lord."* And did not continue to *"the day of vengeance of our God."* Reason? **The purpose of His first coming was to preach salvation to save sinners. When He comes the second time then it shall be *"the vengeance of our God"*. It will be judgment time!**

iii. But this was the day of salvation, the day of accepting and reconciling sinners.

*For he saith, I have heard thee in a time accepted, and in the day of salvation have I succoured thee: behold, now is the accepted time; behold, now is the day of salvation.* (2 Corinthians 6:2)

James and John should have been characterized by the Spirit of Jesus Christ and NOT by vindictiveness!

# CHAPTER 10

# "EDOMITE" CHRISTIANS IN THE CHURCH

**There is a special breed or category of believers in the Church who never give or take forgiveness.** I call them "Edomite" Christians. They never make peace, they feel comfortable keeping malice and enmity with people. Such are described in Scripture,

> *Thus saith the Lord; For three transgressions of Edom, and for four, **I will not turn away the punishment thereof; because he did pursue his brother with the sword, and did cast off all pity, and his anger did tear perpetually, and he kept his wrath forever:*** (Amos 1:11)

The offences committed by Edom are listed,

i. He pursued his brother with the sword,

ii. He cast off all pity;

iii. His anger tore perpetually; and,

iv. He kept his wrath forever.

Edom is accused of relentless persecution,

inhumanity, savage fury and persistent anger. He cast off all pity and like a wild beast, tore his prey which Job aptly describes, *"He teareth me in his wrath"* (Job 16:9).
Christians who are always recollecting and narrating past offences in graphic details and getting very angry and bitter at the same time (as though the offence had just been committed) are like goats which regurgitate their food and chew the cud. To "regurgitate" is to "bring food that had been swallowed, back up into the mouth again."

David talked about what hypocritical mockers did to him in his situation, *"... they gnashed upon me with their teeth"* (Psalms 35:16). They were implacable, brutish enemies who always wished him ill.

GOD'S SENTENCE ON THE UNFORGIVING EDOMITES
God made three pronouncements on Edom –
1. "I will not turn away the punishment thereof..."
2. "I will send fire upon Teman" and
3. "Which shall devour the palaces of Bozrah"

Teman and Bozrah were cities of Edom (Amos 1:11 – 12)

Jesus, teaching on forgiveness said,
(Mark 11:25 – 26)

> 25 ***And when ye stand praying, forgive,*** *if ye have ought against* ***any:*** *that your Father* ***also*** *which is in heaven may forgive you your trespasses.*
> 26 *But* ***if ye do not forgive, neither will your Father*** *which is in heaven* ***forgive your trespasses.***

(Matthew 6:15)

> *But* ***if ye forgive not men their trespasses, neither will your Father forgive your trespasses.***

Describing the unmerciful, the unforgiving and God's judgment on such Paul wrote:
(Romans 1:31 – 32)

> 31 *Without understanding, covenant breakers, without natural affection,* ***implacable, unmerciful:***
> 32 ***Who knowing the judgment of God****, that they which commit such things are worthy of death,* ***not only do the same, but have pleasure in them that do them****.*

"Have pleasure in them that do them!" Yes, so the Bible describes the murderous, wicked ministers and all that encourage their members and friends **never to forgive but rather pray their enemies to death;** people who are influencing others to hate others.

Such are people who recall evils done them in the past for fresh and use them for fiery accusations in the present. Such are described in Proverbs 16:27, *"An evil man diggeth up evil and in his lips there is as a burning fire".*

The Living Bible version explains Romans 1:32 more clearly, it reads, *"They were fully aware of God's death penalty for these crimes, yet they went right ahead and did them anyway and encouraged others to do them, too".*

One of such judgments is listed by the Prophet Hosea,

> *...but the Lord accepteth them not; now will he remember their iniquity, and visit their sins...* (Hosea 8:13)

A clear case of men losing their "pardon"! And their "forgiveness"!! And their "salvation"!!!

# CHAPTER 11

# THE BLOOD OF ABEL VERSUS THE BLOOD OF JESUS

Unforgiveness breeds hatred and malice. It also makes one seek for vengeance. Today we see churches and people praying for their enemies to "die by fire" or "be roasted" or "die in boiling water" or "die by accident", "return to sender" etc. The Bible tells us whose blood is running in their veins when they pray like that – it is the "blood of Abel".

When Cain killed his brother Abel, God said to Cain, **the blood of your brother Abel is crying to me for vengeance.**

(Genesis 4:10 – 11, 15)

> 10 *And he said, What hast thou done? the voice of thy brother's blood crieth unto me from the ground.*
>
> 11 *And now art thou cursed from the earth, which hath opened her mouth to receive thy brother's blood from thy hand;*
>
> 15 *And the Lord said unto him* (Cain), *Therefore*

> *whosoever slayeth Cain, vengeance shall be taken on him sevenfold...*

There was no forgiving. All Abel's blood wanted was vengeance and it got it by the immediate and very severe judgment on Cain! You have "the blood of Abel" in your veins if that is the way you pray.

In contrast, "the Blood of Jesus Christ" speaks better things in that His blood is crying,

> *...Father forgive them for they know not what they do...* (Luke 23:34)
>
> *And to Jesus the mediator of the new covenant, and to* ***the Blood of sprinkling,*** *that* ***speaketh better things*** *than that of Abel.*
> (Hebrews 12:24)

The blood of Jesus speaks "better things": it speaks "forgiveness" and "forgiveness" is nobler than "vengeance". **Everyone that has "the blood of Jesus Christ", everyone who is a child of God, shall speak those "better things" and not speak "vengeance" as "the blood of Abel" speaks.**

"The blood of Abel" speaks for "vengeance", "tit for

tat", "blood for blood", "curse for curse", "an eye for an eye". But "the Blood of Jesus" speaks, "curse not, feed your enemies, do not kill but save, do good to them that hurt you" etc.

> *But I say unto you,* ***Love your enemies, bless*** *them that curse you,* ***do good*** *to them that hate you, and* ***pray for them*** *which despitefully use you, and persecute you;* (Matthew 5:44)

Now consider and ask yourself - Whose "blood" is running in your vein? Is it "that of Abel" or "that of Jesus Christ?"

Everyone praying the "prayer of vengeance" does not have "the blood of Jesus" running through him but "the blood of Abel". If the reVerse were the case, you would pray better prayers.

Run away from "the blood of Abel" that harbours bitterness and hatred in the hearts of people and come to a "better covenant", come to "the Blood of Jesus Christ". Let "the blood of Abel" be drained from your life and "the Blood of Jesus" transfused into you. Become a product of Jesus Christ and not that of Abel!

Jesus says, *"For I have given you an example, that ye should do as I have done to you."* (John 13:15)

LEAVEN OF MALICE AND HATRED

Paul talked about the leaven of malice and hatred which we must take out.

(1 Corinthians 5:7, 8)

> 7 *Purge out therefore the old leaven, that ye may be a new lump, as ye are unleavened. For even Christ our Passover is sacrificed for us:*
>
> 8 *Therefore let us keep the feast, not with old leaven, neither with the leaven of malice and wickedness; but with the unleavened bread of sincerity and truth.*

# CHAPTER 12

## FORGIVING IS NOT FOOLISHNESS OR WEAKNESS

*Because the foolishness of God is wiser than men* (men's wisdom)... (1 Corinthians 1:25)

Are we being foolish when we forgive offences? No! Not at all! In forgiving, we are only following Christ's example.

(1 Peter 2:19 – 23)

19 *For this is thankworthy, if a man for conscience toward God endure grief, suffering wrongfully.*
20 *For what glory is it, if, when ye be buffeted for your faults, ye shall take it patiently? but if, when ye do well, and suffer for it, ye take it patiently, this is acceptable with God.*
21 *For even hereunto were ye called: because Christ also suffered for us, leaving us an example, that ye should follow his steps:*
22 *Who did no sin, neither was guile found in his*

*mouth:*
[23] *Who, when he was reviled, reviled not again; when he suffered, he threatened not; but committed himself to him that judgeth righteously:*

That you forgive an offence may not necessarily mean the offender is right and you wrong. No. By forgiving, you are simply saying to the offender "I am not your judge. I leave matters in the hands of God. Vengeance belongs to Him."

*For we know him that hath said, Vengeance belongeth unto me, I will recompense, saith the Lord. And again, The Lord shall judge his people.* (Hebrews 10:30)

**Neither does doing so portray weakness on your part.**

*Because...the weakness of God is stronger than men.* (1 Corinthians 1:25)

## FORGIVING – EVIDENCE OF STRENGTH

In forgiving, you may look to men weak and foolish but in actual fact you are the stronger and wiser person. When Jesus came down from heaven begging sinners to repent and be forgiven, He was not showing foolishness and weakness, but rather He was showing wisdom, character, love and strength.

> *It is an honour for a man to cease from strife: but every fool will be meddling* (quarrelling). (Proverbs 20:3)

## CONTROLLING ONE'S SPIRIT

Paul, talking about spirits of Christians said, *"The spirits of the prophets are subject to the prophets."* (1 Corinthians 14:32)

**This means, a true Christian in faith is always able to control his spirit, and his temper.** He is strong enough to put his spirit and his emotions under control. He is humble and able to say "I was wrong" when he knows he has offended. On the other hand, those who are proud, self-opinionated and never see themselves as ever doing anything wrong, never accepting blame, are weak people, foolish people. They think themselves wise by not forgiving offences and those who have offended them.

James, talking on "wisdom", made such sobering comparisons between "the wisdom from God" and "the wisdom from the devil".

(James 3:13 – 18)

> 13 *Who is a wise man and endued with knowledge among you? let him shew out of a good conversation his works with meekness of wisdom.*
>
> 14 *But if ye have bitter envying and strife in your hearts, glory not, and lie not against the truth.*
>
> 15 *This wisdom descendeth not from above, but is earthly, sensual, devilish.*
>
> 16 *For where envying and strife is, there is confusion and every evil work.*
>
> 17 *But the wisdom that is from above is first pure, then peaceable, gentle, and easy to be intreated,* (that is, can be easily begged and forgives easily) *full of mercy and good fruits, without partiality, and without hypocrisy.*
>
> 18 *And the fruit of righteousness is sown in peace*

*of them that make peace.*

Take particular note of (Verse 15) *"This wisdom descendeth not from above, but is earthly, sensual, devilish."* We are either filled with The Holy Spirit or we are filled with "spirits of devils". We are advised to, *"Examine yourselves whether ye be in the faith..."* (2 Corinthians 13:5) meaning, check yourself. Are you really a Christian? And if you are, are you still in the faith or backslidden?

Warnings are posted.

> *Pride goeth before destruction, and an haughty spirit before a fall.* (Proverbs 16:18)
>
> *There is a way that seemeth right unto a man, but the end thereof are the ways of death.* (Proverbs 16:25)

**Words Devoid Of Bitterness and Curses Bless Us**

Pleasant words, devoid of curses, are healing therapy. (Proverbs 16:24)

> *Pleasant words are as an honeycomb, sweet to the soul, and health to the bones.*

(Matthew 5:11 – 12)

11 *Blessed are ye, when men shall revile you, and persecute you, and shall say all manner of evil against you falsely, for my sake.*

12 ***Rejoice, and be exceeding glad: for great is your reward in heaven:*** *for so persecuted they the prophets which were before you.*

(1 Peter 3:9)

*Not rendering evil for evil, or railing for railing: but contrariwise blessing; knowing that ye are thereunto called, that ye should* ***inherit a blessing.***

MARKS OF THE TRUE CHRISTIAN

A true Christian is not a hypocrite. A hypocrite is a pretender.

(Romans 12:9 – 14)

9 *Let love be without dissimulation* (be genuine). *Abhor that which is evil; cleave to that which is good.*

10 *Be kindly affectioned one to another with brotherly love;...*

12 *Rejoicing in hope; patient in tribulation;*

*continuing instant in prayer;...*

*[14]Bless them which persecute you: bless, and curse not.*

The true Christian does not go about cursing perceived enemies nor nursing grudges against people in his heart.

Paul advised in Philippians 4:8,

*Finally, brethren, whatsoever things are true, whatsoever things are honest, whatsoever things are just, whatsoever things are pure, whatsoever things are lovely, whatsoever things are of good report; if there be any virtue, and if there be any praise, think on these things.*

A true Christian's thoughts should be pure.

# CHAPTER 13

## CHARACTERISTICS OF A FORGIVING HEART

Teaching on forgiveness in Luke's gospel, Jesus said to His disciples,
(Luke 17:3–4)

> 3 *Take heed to yourselves; if thy brother trespass against thee, rebuke him; and if he repent, forgive him.*
>
> 4 ***And if he trespass against thee seven times in a day** and **seven** times in a day turn again to thee, saying, I repent; thou shalt **forgive** him.*

Thus Jesus wiped out the pre-law "seven-fold" vengeance in Genesis 4:15; (See Chapter Seven)

Following that, Peter asked a question:

> *Then came Peter to him, and said, Lord, how oft shall my brother sin against me, and I forgive him? **Till seven times?*** (Matthew 18:21)

Peter asked this question because based on Luke's account, Jesus had taught that if a person offends you seven times in a day and comes to you seven times to ask for forgiveness, forgive him.

In Matthew 18:22, Jesus gives an answer to Peter,

> ***Jesus saith unto him, I say not unto thee, until seven times; but, until seventy times seven.*** (This simply stands for many times or an unlimited number of times.)

EXPLAINING "SEVEN TIMES SEVEN" AND "SEVENTY TIMES SEVEN"

Saint Luke and Saint Matthew are reporting the same teaching of Jesus Christ on **the number of times we should forgive a repentant offender.** It could be seven times as in Luke (Luke 17:4) or Seventy times Seven as in Matthew (Matthew 18:22). So long as he keeps repenting, he should be forgiven . Thus we cannot put a definite figure to the number of times we could forgive, it cannot be summed up as seven (7) times or seventy times seven (490) times. **Each time forgiveness is given, the offense is wiped out, the slate is clean,** the heart is clean, and free.

7 - 7 = 0

70x7 (490) - 70x7(490) = 0

In summary Jesus taught:
REPENTANCE followed by FORGIVENESS wipes out the record so there is noting to add onto.
By this answer, Jesus **also wiped out or erased the pre-law "seventy and seven fold vengeance"** (Genesis 4:24; Chapter Seven)

Having this response of Jesus in mind, let us study this Scripture concerning the characteristics of a forgiving heart:

(Ephesians 4:31, 32)

> 31 *Let all bitterness, and wrath, and anger, and clamor, and evil speaking, be put away from you, with all malice:*
> 32 *And be ye kind one to another, tenderhearted, forgiving one another, even as God for Christ's sake hath forgiven you.*

1. **A Forgiving Heart is always forgiving**

The word used is "forgiving" and **not** "forgive". This is a "present continuous tense" implying "**continuously forgiving**" one another.

2. **"Tenderhearted"**

Another word there is "Tenderhearted", **that is, a heart that can be entreated, a heart that accepts apologies when people say, "I am sorry"**. A "hard heart", a "stony heart" does not accept "I am sorry". It is a heart that is "soft", a heart that is "tender" that can overlook offence, and so is able to be forgiving any time someone says, "I am sorry".

For some of us, our temperament is so sharp that at the slightest offence, it sparks off; we are hot tempered – little offences tick us off, our threshold of tolerance is very low. The cure for that kind of sharp temper is tenderness, tender-heartedness.

For an illustration, if I throw an inflated ball on a stony ground or hard surface, the ball bounces back up, for the simple reason of hardness of the surface. The surface "rejects" the ball so to say. But if I take that same ball and drop it on a mud floor (soft ground), it will attempt to bounce back but cannot because of the muddy soft ground. The mud will "hold" it and prevent it from jumping back. It will just "arrest" the ball, "absorb" the ball, "embrace" the ball.

In the same manner, when a heart is as hard as a rock, nothing stays there. Because it is so sensitive, so temperamental, anything that touches the heart, even a mere joke, sparks it off. The hard heart will reject peace moves; the hard heart will never forgive an offence! But when the heart is soft like mud, when offences are thrown at it, it does not spark off, it just absolves them because it is a tender, soft heart.

Our prayer should be that God will give us tender and soft hearts; that our hard hearts be made soft and tender.

3. **"Forbearing One Another"**

*__Forbearing one another__, and forgiving one another, if any man have a quarrel against any: even as Christ forgave you, __so also do ye__.* (Colossians 3:13)

**"Forbearing one another" means, "tolerating one another".** Tolerance means, the willingness to accept or tolerate opinions or behavior that you may not agree with, or people who are not like you. This we must always remember, that people are created differently.

4. **"Follow Peace"**

*Flee also youthful lust; but* ***follow*** *righteousness, faith, charity,* ***peace,*** *with them that call on the Lord out of a pure heart.* (2 Timothy 2:22)

There are four things we are asked to "follow" in this passage:

i. Righteousness
ii. Faith
iii. Charity (Love) and
iv. Peace

**Do not let them desert you or go behind you. Follow** them very diligently. Wherever they go, follow! **"Follow"** means **"to come or go after or behind"**. Be a follower of peace. In the matter of offences, be a "follower" not a "leader". "Peace" going ahead, will douse the flame before your arrival!

If your enemies are not available or nearby, track them call them, talk to them and forgive them - for your own sake!

# CHAPTER 14

# PURITY OF HEART

The Bible says so much about the state or condition of our hearts and how that affects our relationship with God and man.

In Matthew 5:8 we have the sixth beatitude, *"Blessed are the* ***pure*** *in heart; for* ***they shall see God".*** This was briefly treated in Chapter Five, Number 6.

In Psalms 24:3 – 4, a question is asked in Verse 3 and answered in Verse 4.

> 3 *Who shall* ***ascend into the hill of the Lord****? or* ***who shall stand in his holy place?***
>
> 4 *He that* ***hath*** *clean hands, and a* ***pure heart;*** *who hath not lifted up his soul unto vanity, nor sworn deceitfully.*

The blessing of the Lord is not just His benefits, it is His Presence as well.

(Numbers 6:24 – 26)

> 24 *The Lord bless thee, and keep thee:*

> 25 *The Lord make his face shine upon thee, and be gracious unto thee:*
> 26 *The Lord lift up his countenance upon thee, and give thee peace.*

1. "The Lord bless you" – "Benefit".
2. "Keep you" – "His Presence".
3. "The Lord make His face shine upon you" – "His Presence".
4. "Be gracious to you" – "Benefit".
5. "The Lord lift up His countenance upon you" – "His Presence".
6. "Give you peace" – "Benefit".

In all three Verses of this Scripture, His Presence is what brings His benefits and the blessings. And what brings His presence are holiness and purity of heart, hearts that do not bear grudges, hearts that are not locked against anyone, hearts that are open, hearts that have "put away all malice." (Ephesians 4:31); hearts that are no longer *"living in malice and envy, hateful, and hating one another."* (Titus 3:3)

To be welcomed into the Presence of the Lord is a

mighty blessing in itself. In God's presence, there is fullness of joy, at His right hand there are pleasures for evermore (Psalms 16:11). His presence affords rest (Exodus 33:14). His presence gives courage in life's battles (Deuteronomy 20:1). His presence gives comfort in trials (Psalms 43:2). On the other hand, to be turned away from His Presence is misery and death (Proverbs 1:30 – 33; 21:16).

> *The thoughts of the wicked are an abomination to the Lord; but the words of the pure are pleasant words* (to the Lord). (Proverbs 15:26)

**Two Examples of Those Who Craved For the Presence of the Lord**

1. **Moses**

   Moses craved for the presence of the Lord.

   *And he said unto Him, **If thy presence go not with me,** carry us not up hence.* (Exodus 33:15)

*Result:And He said, **My presence shall go with thee,** and **I will give thee rest**.* (Exodus 33:14)

2. **David**

   David pleaded not to be cast away.

***Cast me not away from thy presence;*** *and take not Thy Holy Spirit from me.* (Psalms 51:11)

Result: *Thou compasseth my path and my lying down, and art acquinted with all my ways.* (Psalms 139:3)

**Two Examples of What Happened to Those Who Went out Of God's Presence**

1. **Cain**

Cain "went out" of the presence of the Lord.

*And* ***Cain went out from the presence of the Lord,*** *and dwelt in the land of Nod, on the east of Eden.* (Genesis 4:16)

Consequence: Cain became a wanderer with no permanent place of abode.

2. **Judas Iscariot**

Judas Iscariot **went out of the Presence of the Lord**

*He then* ***having received the sop went immediately out:*** *and it was night.* (John 13:30)

Consequence: He destroyed himself and missed heaven.

*And he cast down the pieces of silver in the temple, and departed, and went and hanged himself.* (Matthew 27:5)

*Now this man purchased a field with the reward of iniquity; and falling headlong, he burst asunder in the midst, and all his bowels gushed out.* (Acts 1:18)

*The backslider in heart shall be filled with his own ways.* (Proverbs 14:14a)

**Other Blessings in His Presence**

a. Glory and Honour

*Glory and honour are in his presence; strength and gladness are in his place.*

(1 Chronicles 16:27)

b. Fullness Of Joy

*...In thy Presence is fullness of joy...*

(Psalms 16:11)

c. A Place Of Hiding

*Thou shalt hide them in the secret of Thy presence from the pride of man: thou shalt keep them secretly in a pavilion from the strife of tongues.* (Psalms 31:20)

**Only The Upright Can Dwell in His Presence**

*...the upright shall dwell in thy Presence.*
(Psalms 140:13)

**The Wicked Are Cast Out**

On the other hand the wicked are cast out from His Presence *"... He had cast them out from his presence"* (Jeremiah 52:3)

In summary, two conditions are now announced, as seen in Psalms 24:4

> *He that hath clean hands, and a pure heart; who hath not lifted up his soul unto vanity, nor sworn deceitfully.*

First, the one welcomed to His holy Presence is the one "who has clean hands". Second, the one welcomed to His holy Presence is the one "who has a pure heart".

The heart is made impure by evil thoughts.
(Matthew 15:19 – 20)

> 19 *For out of the heart proceed evil thoughts, murders, adulteries, fornications, thefts, false*

*witness, blasphemies:*

*[20]These are the things which defile a man: but to eat with unwashen hands defileth not a man.*

In the book of Proverbs it is summarized this way: (Proverbs 1:30 – 33)

***[30]They would none of my counsel: they despised all my reproof.***

*[31]Therefore shall they eat of the fruit of their own way, and be filled with their own devices.*

*[32]For the turning away of the simple shall slay them, and the prosperity of fools shall destroy them.*

*[33]But whoso hearkeneth unto me shall dwell safely, and shall be quiet from fear of evil.*

Listen to the pure Word of God, not the contrived one, and you shall not be afraid or live in fear and ever always suspecting people!

Psalms 91:5 says, *"Thou shalt not be afraid for the terror by night; nor for the arrow that flieth by day;"* Psalms 112:7 says, *"He shall not be afraid of evil tidings: his heart is fixed, trusting in the Lord."*

Proverbs 3:24 says, *"When thou liest down, thou shalt not be afraid: yea, thou shalt lie down, and thy sleep shall be sweet."* and Hebrews 13:6 says *"So that we may boldly say, The Lord is my helper, and I will not fear what man shall do unto me."*

WORKS OF THE FLESH – ETERNAL SEPARATION FROM GOD

Galatians 5:19 – 21 enumerates the works of the flesh and the consequences that follow the life of the flesh:

> [19] *Now the works of the flesh are manifest, which are these; Adultery, fornication, uncleanness, lasciviousness,*
> [20] *Idolatry, witchcraft, hatred, variance, emulations, wrath, strife, seditions, heresies,*
> [21] *Envyings, murders, drunkenness, revellings, and such like: of the which I tell you before, as I have also told you in time past, that they which do such things shall not inherit the kingdom of God.*

Listed amongst them are **'hatred'**, **'variance'**, **'emulations'**, **'wrath'**, **'strife'**, **'seditions'**, **'envyings'**, **'murders'**.

**Consequences of Separation from God**

> *...of the which I tell you before, as I have also told you in time past, that they which do such things shall not inherit the kingdom of God.*
> (Galatians 5:21)

It is either heaven or hell. If you do not make heaven, you will definitely make hell. Why? Because you prefer to live the life of the flesh!

Paul admonishes,

(Galatians 5:13 – 15)

> 13 *For, brethren, ye have been called unto liberty; only use not liberty for an occasion to the flesh, but by love serve one another.*
> 14 *For all the law is fulfilled in one word, even in this; Thou shalt love thy neighbour as thyself.*
> 15 *But if ye bite and devour one another, take heed that ye be not consumed one of another.*

(Galatians 6:8)

> *For he that soweth to his flesh shall of the flesh reap corruption; but he that soweth to the Spirit shall of the Spirit reap life everlasting.*

We reap what we sow. He who sows to the flesh, who indulges his sensual and animal appetites, shall have corruption as the crop he will reap. You cannot expect to lead a bad life and go to heaven at last.

FRUIT OF THE SPIRIT: ETERNAL LIFE

On the other hand, Galatians 5:18 talks about those who are led by the Holy Spirit – *"But if ye be led by the Spirit, ye are not under the law"*. Such people bear the fruit of the Spirit – 'love', 'joy', 'peace', 'longsuffering', 'gentleness', 'goodness', 'faith', 'meekness', 'temperance' *against which there is no law* (that is, there is no law against these).
(Galatians 5:22 – 23)

> 22*But the fruit of the Spirit is love, joy, peace, longsuffering, gentleness, goodness, faith,*
> 23*Meekness, temperance: against such there is no law.*

**Blessings of bearing the fruit of the Spirit**

> *...but he that soweth to the Spirit shall of the Spirit reap life everlasting.* (Galatians 6:8)

According as your present life is, so will be your eternal life. Whether your sowing be to the flesh or to the Spirit, so will your eternal reaping be. To reap signifies enjoyment and happiness or punishment in another world. He who trusts in Christ and receives the gifts and graces of the Holy Spirit, shall reap life everlasting.

**We are urged to prove our work**
(Galatians 6:4 – 5)

> [4] *But let every man prove his own work, and then shall he have rejoicing in himself alone, and not in another.*
>
> [5] *For every man shall bear his own burden.*

**We must learn to govern our spirits** *"...the spirits of the prophet are subject to the prophets."* (1 Corinthians 14:32).

The man who takes fire at every offence, whose eyes flash with rage, and lips mutter threats is sowing to the flesh *"...hatred, variance, wrath (anger), strife..."* (Galatians 5:20 – 21) and shall not inherit the Kingdom of God.

# CHAPTER 15

# FORGIVENESS OR FORGIVING – NOT EASY

Forgiveness or forgiving is not easy because it is not in man's nature to forgive. It is a divine attribute. This much we learn from the request made by the Apostles and from personal experience.

Jesus said to His disciples,
(Luke 17:3 – 4)

> 3 *Take heed to yourselves: If thy brother trespass against thee,* ***rebuke him*** (that is, tell him he has offended you)*; and if he repent, forgive him.*
> 4 *And if he trespass against thee seven times in a day, and seven times in a day turn again to thee, saying,* ***I repent****; thou shalt* ***forgive him.***

**Increase of Faith**

On hearing this teaching, His disciples made a request of him.

> *And the apostles said unto the Lord, Increase our faith.* (Luke 17:5)

Forgiveness is so difficult, that it requires a new level of faith! So when we are able to forgive, it is a sign that our faith is growing! We must therefore seek divine help to enable us to forgive. That was what the disciples did; they asked for increase of faith.

FAITH TESTED

Our faith must be tested to know how much or how far it has grown.

**Instruments of Testing**

The Scriptures list some of the instruments of testing of our faith.

1. "School Masters"

   (Galatians 3:24 – 25)

   24 *Wherefore the law was our schoolmaster to bring us unto Christ, that we might be justified by faith.*

   25 *But after that faith is come, we are no longer under a schoolmaster.*

2. Tribulations

   *...and exhorting them to continue in the faith, and that we must through much tribulation*

*enter into the kingdom of God.* (Acts 14:22)

**Benefits of Trial of Faith**

- Praise, Honour, Glory

  *That the trial of your faith, being much more precious than of gold that perisheth, though it be tried with fire, might be found unto praise and honour and glory at the appearing of Jesus Christ:* (1 Peter 1:7)

- Equipped For Counselling

  *For in that he himself hath suffered being tempted, he is able to succour them that are tempted.* (Hebrews 2:18)

People that are offending us are serving useful purposes in our lives for now and for eternity after all! By their offences, they are increasing our faith if we are able to overlook their offences and forgive them seventy times seven times! In fact we should thank them and bless them!

> *But I say unto you, Love your enemies, bless them that curse you, do good to them that hate you, and pray for them which despitefully use you, and persecute you;* (Matthew 5:44)

*Bless them that curse you, and pray for them which despitefully use you.* (Luke 6:28)

# CHAPTER 16

# AID TO FORGIVENESS

1. INCREASE IN FAITH

This we have read in Chapter Fifteen but for purposes of emphasis it is recalled here.

When Jesus told them to forgive all the time they exclaimed, "God, who can do so?" And they prayed this prayer, "Please Lord help us. Increase our faith." Forgiveness is not an easy thing to give especially when you have been hurt terribly. When we find it difficult to forgive, let us pray for increase of our faith.

The One that will increase our faith is the Holy Spirit. So, if we forgive, we will be pleasing the Holy Spirit, and He will be available to increase our faith.

2. "SOWING" PEACE

(James 3:13 – 18)

13 *Who is a wise man and endued with knowledge*

*among you? let him shew out of a good conversation his works with meekness of wisdom.*
14 *But if ye have bitter envying and strife in your hearts, glory not, and lie not against the truth.*
15 *This wisdom descendeth not from above, but is earthly, sensual, devilish (it is from the devil).*
16 *For where envying and strife is, there is confusion and every evil work.*
17 *But the wisdom that is from above is first pure, then peaceable, gentle, and easy to be intreated, full of mercy and good fruits, without partiality, and without hypocrisy.*
18 *And the fruit of righteousness is* ***sown in peace*** *of them that make peace.*

James talks about "the fruit of righteousness". Righteousness is a fruit that we reap when we sow peace. And the seed of peace is sown only in them that make peace. You might be praying for the Holy Spirit to baptize you. This is only possible for those who make peace. The fruit of the Spirit will not grow in you if you are the quarrelsome, fighting, unforgiving, hating person. Like any other seed that is sown, "peace-seed" needs a peaceful, quiet and undisturbed soil (heart) to grow and to bear the fruit of righteousness. Therefore beloved, Paul urges,

> *...be not conformed to this world: but be ye transformed by the renewing of your mind, that ye may prove what is that good, and acceptable, and perfect, will of God.* (Romans 12:2)

David cried, *"Create in me a clean heart, O God; and renew a right spirit within me."* (Psalms 51:10)

People who are hot-tempered, flash tempered and unforgiving, do not keep friendship for long. If they do, it has to be on their own terms. Such are asked to pray, *"...that we may lead a quiet and peaceable life in all godliness and honesty. For this is good and acceptable in the sight of God our Saviour;"*
(1 Timothy 2:2, 3)

And in the Beatitude Jesus taught, ***"Blessed are the peacemakers: for they shall be called the children of God."*** (Matthew 5:9)
The book of Proverbs says,

*Deceit is in the heart of them that imagine evil: but to the counsellors of peace is joy.* (Proverbs 12:20)

Paul urges again,

*Let us therefore follow after* ***the things which make for peace****, and things wherewith one may edify another.* (Romans 14:19)

*Let nothing be done through strife or vainglory; but in lowliness of mind let each esteem other better than themselves.* (Philippians 2:3)

3. GRACE

**We are enabled to forgive by grace.** Grace is

i. Beneficence or generosity shown by God to man.

ii. It also means, "disposition to kindness, favour, clemency or compassion." (Webster's dictionary)

In both the Old Testament and the New Testament, the Bible speaks eloquently about **GRACE**. A few Bible references are here given:

*...and he shall bring forth the headstone thereof*

*with shoutings, crying, Grace, grace unto it.* (Zechariah 4:7)

*For the law was given by Moses, but grace and truth came by Jesus Christ.* (John 1:17)

*But we believe that through the grace of the Lord Jesus Christ we shall be saved, even as they.* (Acts 15:11)

*Being justified freely by his grace through the redemption that is in Christ Jesus.*
(Romans 3:24)

*For the grace of God that bringeth salvation hath appeared to all men.* (Titus 2:11)

There is a song in appreciation of Grace.

Oh the love that drew salvation's plan;
Oh the Grace that brought it down to man;
Oh the mighty gulf that God did span at Calvary.
Mercy there was great and grace was free,
**Pardon there was multiplied to me;**
There my burdened soul found liberty at Calvary.

Jesus Christ alone saves and His grace enables our heart and mind to forgive and to pardon all men.

# CHAPTER 17

# FORGIVENESS IN THE CHURCH: THOSE WHO ASK FOR PARDON AND FORGIVENESS

Offenders are in two categories: those **who will ask for forgiveness** and those **who will not ask for forgiveness.** There are three places we meet offenders. We meet them in the Church (brethren), we meet them in the public (unbelievers) and we meet them in the family.

(Luke 17: 3 – 4)

> [3]*Take heed to yourselves: If thy brother trespass against thee,* ***rebuke him*** (tell him); *and if he repent, forgive him.*
>
> [4]*And if he trespass against thee seven times in a day, and seven times in a day turn again to thee, saying, I repent; thou shalt forgive him.*

William MacDonald comments:

> "In the Christian life there is not only the peril of offending others. There is also the danger of harbouring grudges, of refusing to forgive when an offending person apologizes. That is what The Lord deals with here."

(Believer's Bible Commentary, William MacDonald, 1995)

The New Testament teaches the following procedure in connection with this subject:

1. If a Christian is wronged by another Christian, **he should first of all forgive the offender in his heart.** *"... if ye from your hearts forgive not everyone his brother their trespasses"* (Matthew 18:35). This keeps his own soul free from resentment and malice.

2. Then **he should go to the offender privately to discuss the offense.**

   *"...go and tell him his fault between thee and him* ***alone".*** (Matthew 18:15)

3. **If he repents**

   *"...If he shall hear thee..."* (Matthew 18:15) meaning, if he admits his fault. James says, *"Admit your faults one to another..."* (James 5:16 - The Living Bible)

4. *"Thou shalt forgive him"* (Luke 17:4) He should be told (from the mouth) that he is forgiven. Matthew says *"...thou hast gained thy brother"* (Matthew 18:15)

5. When peace is thus brokered, it should be iced with prayer *"...and pray one for another..."* (James 5:16)

The Bible encourages Christians to forgive, to always forgive, and to be ready to forgive.

> *And be ye kind one to another, tender hearted,* ***forgiving*** (present continuous) *one another, even as God for Christ's sake hath forgiven you.* (Ephesians 4:32)

> ***Forbearing*** *one another, and* ***forgiving*** *one another, if any man have a quarrel against any:*

> *even as Christ forgave you, so also do ye.* (Colossians 3:13)

The purpose of going to tell the person who offended you (Matthew 18:15) is not to get even, not to have an opportunity to start a new quarrel, not to continue from where the last one ended or to humiliate the offender, but to restore fellowship with him and both of you together with God.

# CHAPTER 18

# FORGIVENESS IN THE CHURCH: THOSE WHO REBUFF PEACE EFFORTS

In times of misunderstandings and quarrels, there are certain people both in and out of the Church who rebuff peace efforts.

David had said, *"My soul hath long dwelt with him that hateth peace. I am for peace: but when I speak, they are for war."* (Psalms 120:6-7). Some people are like that. They are always on the war path. The way of peace they know not. **They will never accept blame, never make peace, they will never apologize neither do they accept apology from people who have offended them including brethren. They never forgive neither do they accept forgiveness when offered.** The Bible describes such people in Romans 3:17 – 18: *"...the way of peace have they not known: There is no fear of God before their eyes."* They are in permanent state of war and animosity and they enjoy it; they feel "comfortable" with things staying that way. What to do with such people? Ask God to deliver them as well as you from being bitter against them. This kind of people are the type Jesus is alluding to in Matthew 18:21–22 when Peter asked his question on forgiveness.

> 21 *Then came Peter to him, and said, Lord, how oft shall my brother sin against me, and I forgive him? till seven times?*
>
> 22 *Jesus saith unto him, I say not unto thee, Until seven times: but, Until seventy times seven* (that is indefinitely).

STAGES OF A PEACE EFFORT IN THE CHURCH WITH DIFFICULT BRETHREN

Prescribed below are the steps of Biblical peace efforts in the Church for those who rebuff peace efforts; those who would not want to make peace. (Matthew 18:15 – 20)

> 15 *Moreover, if thy brother* (that is your Christian brother) *shall trespass against thee, go and tell him his fault between thee and him alone: if he shall hear thee, thou hast gained thy brother.*
>
> 16 *But if he will not hear; thee, then take with thee*

*one or two more, that in the mouth of two or three witnesses every word may be established.*

[17]*And if he shall neglect to hear them, tell it unto the Church: but if he neglect to hear the Church, let him be unto thee as an heathen man and a publican.*

[18]*Verily I say unto you, Whatsoever ye shall bind on earth shall be bound in heaven; and whatsoever ye shall loose on earth shall be loosed in heaven.*

[19]*Again I say unto you if two of you shall agree on earth as touching anything that they shall ask it shall be done for of my Father which is in heaven.*

[20]*For where two or three are gathered together in my name, there am I in the midst of them.*

**Step 1 – "You Go Alone and Tell Him Privately"**

Jesus teaches the first step is, you go alone and privately tell the person the offence or the wrong done you (Verse 15). He may not even know he had offended you! Go privately and tell him that he had offended you and that you have not been happy with him.

This is what Jesus wants done in His Church. Brothers, sisters, go to the person you are not happy with, go and tell that person the wrong done you. The emphasis is **you** going. **You,** not the offender, taking the initiative for peace.

This is one area we are failing in the Church. We are not able to go to the person we are offended with and to tell him "Look brother, you offended me in this or that area". We will rather keep quiet; keep it in our heart and begin to hold grudges, nurse grudges against the person. We are being taught in this Verse that the first step is, ***"Go and tell him"*** his fault between you and him alone. That is the Bible sequence or order.

The second aspect of that Verse 15 says, *"If he shall hear thee, thou hast gained thy brother."* What this simply means is that if you tell him and he says, "Oh, I did not know that I offended you. I am sorry", you have gained your brother, that is, you have won your brother over. Perhaps, because of the offence you were not communicating with him or relating with him anymore but by reason of his apology and you forgiving, you have now gained him or her, both of you can now pray together, move together again, talk together and do things together again freely instead of being one mile apart.

**This private visit** is not limited to **one** "going". It could be several **"goings"** before peace is achieved!

**Step 2 – "Take One or Two Brothers or Sisters Along"**

The second major step is found in Verse 16: *"But if he will not hear thee..."* There are people like that; people who are hard-hearted and do not want peace.

When you go to them and say, "Look, you offended me." Rather than being sorry, they will shout at you, "What do you mean? Me? Who is the offender, you or me? In any case, who gave you the boldness to come and talk to me? Don't you know who I am? What exactly do you mean? etc". And instead of peace, the misunderstanding would even grow worse than what it was before. It escalates.
Again there are others who, when you approach for peace; they will not say one word to you! You will

plead and plead yet they will be silent. Because they are locked inside their hearts, they would not say a word to you. Tired, you walk away without achieving the peace you went to make. The Bible says you should not be discouraged by this attitude because you are pursing peace. Peace is a runner, it runs away from us! Hence the Bible says pursue it.

> *Let him eschew evil, and do good; let him seek peace, and ensue it.* (1 Peter 3:11)

**Follow Peace**

> *Follow peace with all men, and holiness, without which no man shall see the Lord:*
> (Hebrews 12:14).
> Be a *"follow follow"* (slang, meaning, following sheepishly or foolishly)

The Bible says to take along with you a brother or sister and say to him or her, "Please come, I want to make peace with this sister or this brother. I have gone myself alone; he/she refused to listen to me. Please, join me let us go, so I can plead again before you".

> *...then take with thee one or two more, that in*

*the mouth of two or three witnesses every word may be established.* (Verse 16)

This second step is also not limited to one visit. It could be several visits before peace is brokered. You are to take along "one or two persons" for two purposes:

a. **To join you in pleading for peace**
*And if he shall neglect to hear them...* (Verse 17)
*"Hear them"* means that as you go with that second person, that person will also join you to plead. So it is not you alone pleading anymore. The person will say, "Sister, or brother, if somebody begs you to make peace, you should forgive. Please for Christ's sake, forgive."

b. **As a witness to your peace efforts**
*...that in the mouth of two or three witnesses every word may be established.* (Verse 16)

The second person will be a witness. And we shall see where that witness will come in pretty soon. You will need a witness because the case will soon go to court, the Ecclesiastical court – the court of the Church. And, to prove your case, you need to take along a witness.

If that person's heart is still hardened and he or she will not forgive you, you and your witness should gently go your way. But that is still not the end of the peace effort. There is one more step to take, one more effort to make.

**Step 3- Tell it to the Church: The Ecclesiastical Court**

The third stage is found in Verse 17 *"And if he shall neglect to hear them, tell it unto the Church."*

The third step is to go and tell the authority of your Church. This authority refers to the Pastors and Elders (not the general congregation).

If she or he still refuses to hear the Church authority, the Church will then call you to come along with your witness to testify before her (one of the duties of Elders is to make peace between and amongst brethren).

The case is now in the Court of the Church and of course, the Church (Ecclesiastical) court is higher than the worldly court. The Church will now hear the case. Remember what the Bible says in Matthew 18:20: *"Where two or three of you are gathered in my Name there am I in their midst."* So, when the court is summoned and your case is presented for judgment by the Church, God, Jesus Himself, will be present and He is the Chief Judge of that court.

The Ecclesiastical court has more authority than the Supreme Court of any land. We Christians should not take cases between and amongst us to the worldly Courts, but to the Court of the Church, the Ecclesiastical Court.

In 1 Corinthians 6:1 – 6 we are warned,

> 1 *Dare any of you, having a matter against another, go to law before the unjust, and not before the saints?*
> 2 *Do ye not know that the saints shall judge the world? and if the world shall be judged by you, are ye unworthy to judge the smallest matters?*
> 3 *Know ye not that we shall judge angels? how much more things that pertain to this life?*

> [4] *If then ye have judgments of things pertaining to this life, set them to judge who are least esteemed in the church.*
> [5] *I speak to your shame. Is it so, that there is not a wise man among you? no, not one that shall be able to judge between his brethren?*
> [6] *But brother goeth to law with brother, and that before the unbelievers.*

The Church will hear both sides and apportion blame appropriately.

### Step 4 – The Ecclesiastical Supreme Court and Excommunication

The Ecclesiastical Court, the court in the Church is the Appeal Court of Heaven here on earth. Every case is heard at the Appeal Court, before it goes to the Supreme Court.

If after being heard in the Appeal Court and the sister's or brother's heart remains adamant and she or he says, "Hmm, my Pastor, I respect you; my Elders, I respect you all, but you see this case? We are going to judge it in heaven." Some determined unforgiving hardhearted Christians actually say that sometimes!

## Excommunication

If this is the case, this is what will happen: The consequence on such a person will be terrible. The Church will pronounce and declare him or her an unbeliever and a heathen.

> *And if he shall neglect to hear them, tell it unto the church: but if he neglect to hear the church, let him be unto thee as an heathen man and a publican.* (Matthew 18:17)

The Church will declare such a pagan and excommunicate such. It does not matter who they are or how spiritual they may be, etc. If the Church declares such an infidel or an unbeliever, it stands, and automatically excludes him/her from the Church here on earth, as well as from heaven.

> *Verily I say unto you, Whatsoever ye shall bind on earth shall be bound in heaven; and whatsoever ye shall loose on earth shall be loosed in heaven.* (Matthew 18:18)
>
> *Now we command you, brethren, in the name of our Lord Jesus Christ that ye withdraw yourselves from every brother* (and sister) *that walketh disorderly, and not after the tradition which he received of us.* (2 Thessalonians 3:6)

Such are out of fellowship of the Church on earth and out of the fellowship in heaven.

> *Again I say unto you, That if two of you shall agree on earth as touching anything that they shall ask, it shall be done for them of my Father which is in heaven.* (Matthew 18:19)

In other words, the Church's pronouncement will be accepted and executed by heaven and in heaven! That is how serious God views unforgiveness! That is why Jesus Christ Himself urges us to make peace and make it quickly because the opportunity for doing so could be lost if for an example, one of the party dies. If that happens, you are stuck!

(Matthew 5:25 – 26)

> 25 *Agree with thine adversary quickly, whiles thou art in the way with him; lest at any time the adversary deliver thee to the judge, and the judge deliver thee to the officer, and thou be cast into prison.*
>
> 26 *Verily I say unto thee, Thou shalt by no means come out thence, till thou hast paid the uttermost farthing.*

Proverbs 14:12 says, *"There is a way that seemeth right unto a man, but the end thereof are the ways of death."*

## Nobody Is Bigger Than the Church

The Church has authority and no individual is bigger than the Church or can hold the Church to ransom! Let us consider the case of Ananias and Sapphira in Acts 5:1 – 11.

*1 But a certain man named Ananias, with Sapphira his wife, sold a possession,*

*2 And kept back part of the price, his wife also being privy to it, and brought a certain part, and laid it at the apostles' feet.*

*3 But Peter said, Ananias, why hath Satan filled thine heart to lie to the Holy Ghost, and to keep back part of the price of the land?*

*4 Whiles it remained, was it not thine own? And after it was sold, was it not in thine own power? Why hast thou conceived this thing in thine heart? Thou hast not lied unto men, but unto God.*

*5 And Ananias hearing these words fell down, and gave up the ghost: and great fear came on*

*all them that heard these things.*
6 *And the young men arose, wound him up, and carried him out, and buried him.*
7 *And it was about the space of three hours after, when his wife, not knowing what was done, came in.*
8 *And Peter answered unto her, Tell me whether ye sold the land for so much? And she said, Yea, for so much.*
9 *Then Peter said unto her, How is it that ye have agreed together to tempt the Spirit of the Lord? Behold, the feet of them which have buried thy husband are at the door, and shall carry thee out.*
10 *Then fell she down straightway at his feet, and yielded up the ghost: and the young men came in, and found her dead, and, carrying her forth, buried her by her husband.*
11 *And great fear came upon all the church, and upon as many as heard these things.*

They were a wealthy couple and they promised their land to the Church. They sold it but brought only part of the money to the Church.

Peter asked, "Is that all you sold the land for?" The husband said "Yes". Peter said to him "you have lied unto the Holy Spirit", and immediately he fell down and died (Verses 4 – 5).

When his wife came later and told the same lie (Verse 7 – 10), she also was struck dead, and these "pillars" of the first Church, financial pillars, important pillars in the Church, in one fell swoop, were destroyed out of the Church. Their being financiers of the early Church notwithstanding, they were taken out. The Church leaders preferred to miss out on their money rather than to lose the Church by allowing the seed of sin to be sown which like leaven, would have eventually grown and polluted the entire Church. The purified early Church rather than reduce in number, multiplied tremendously!

> *And believers were the more added to the Lord, multitudes both of men and women.* (Acts 5:14)

The Church did not collapse because these rich people were no longer there. The Church moved on to higher ground, stronger and healthier.

(Acts 5:15 – 16)

> [15] *Insomuch that they brought forth the sick into the streets, and laid them on beds and couches, that at the least the shadow of Peter passing by might overshadow some of them.*
>
> [16] *There came also a multitude out of the cities round about unto Jerusalem, bringing sick folks, and them which were vexed with unclean spirits: and they were healed every one.*

Nobody holds the Church of Jesus Christ to ransom, nobody! I beg every one of you; begin to revere the Church and her authority. Do not play with the Church. Do not talk lightly about the Church.

# CHAPTER 19

# FORGIVING THE WORLD (THE UNBELIEVERS)

In the matter of loving and forgiving the people of the world, several Scriptures readily come to mind beginning with the very statements of Jesus on this subject matter.

(Matthew 5:43–48)

43 *Ye have heard that it hath been said, Thou shalt love thy neighbour, and hate thine enemy.*

44 *But I say unto you, Love your enemies, bless them that curse you, do good to them that hate you, and pray for them which despitefully use you, and persecute you;*

45 *That ye may be the children of your Father which is in heaven: for he maketh his sun to rise on the evil and on the good, and sendeth rain on the just and on the unjust.*

46 *For if ye love them which love you, what reward have ye? do not even the publicans the*

*same?*
47 *And if ye salute your brethren only, what do ye more than others? do not even the publicans so?*
48 *Be ye therefore perfect, even as your Father which is in heaven is perfect.*

William MacDonald's Bible Commentary on these Verses explain these Verses of Scripture clearly.

"Our Lord's final example of the higher righteousness demanded in His Kingdom concerns the treatment of one's enemies. The Law had taught the Israelites to love their neighbour (Leviticus 19:18). Although they were never explicitly commanded to hate their enemy, this spirit underlay much of their indoctrination. This attitude was a summary of the Old Testament's outlook toward those who persecuted God's people. (Psalms 139:21, 22)

21 *Do not I hate them, O Lord, that hate thee? and am not I grieved with those that rise up against thee?*
22 *I hate them with perfect hatred: I count them mine enemies.*

It was a righteous hostility directed against the enemies of God (I here also add, hostility directed at the individuals). *"...therefore shall I* ***see my desire*** *upon them that hate me."* (Psalms 118:7)

But now Jesus announces that we are to love our enemies and to pray for those who persecute us (Matthew 5:44 – 47). The fact that love is commanded shows that it is a matter of the will and not primarily of the emotions. It is not the same as natural affection because it is not natural to love those who hate and harm you. It is a supernatural grace and can be manifested only by those who have divine life.

There is no reward if we love those who love us. Jesus says that even unconverted tax collectors do that! That type of love requires no divine power. Neither is there any virtue in greeting our brethren only. The unsaved can do that; there is nothing distinctively Christian about that. If our standards are no higher than the world's, it is certain that we will never make an impact on the world. Jesus said His followers should return good for evil so that they might be sons of their Father in heaven (Matthew 5:45). He was not saying that this was the way to become sons of God; rather it is how we show that we are God's children. Since God shows no partiality to either the evil or the good (in that both benefit from sun and rain) (Matthew 5:45). So we should deal graciously and fairly with all.

Jesus closes this section with the admonition:

> *Therefore you shall be perfect, just as your Father in heaven is perfect.*
> (Matthew 5: 48 - New King James Version)

The word **perfect** must be understood in the light of the context. It does **not** mean sinless or flawless. The previous Verses explain that to be perfect means to love those who hate us, to pray for those who persecute us, and to show kindness to both friend and foe. Perfection here is that spiritual maturity which enables a Christian to imitate God in dispensing blessing to everybody without partiality." (Emphasis mine)

(Believer's Bible Commentary, William MacDonald, 1995)

Forgiving is something that we are required to do all the time, in all of our life.

> *And be ye kind one to another, tenderhearted, forgiving one another, even as God for Christ's sake hath forgiven you.* (Ephesians 4:32)
>
> *Forbearing one another, and forgiving one another, if any man have a quarrel against any: even as Christ forgave you, so also do ye.* (Colossians 3:13)

HEART-FORGIVENESS

In all of this forgiving, whether within the fold or outside the fold, our hearts must be involved.

> *So likewise shall my heavenly Father do also unto you, if ye from your hearts forgive not everyone his brother their trespasses.* (Matthew 18:35)

"The goodness and indulgence of God toward us are the pattern we should follow in our dealings with others." (Adam Clarke's Commentary, 1972)

"The application is clear. God is the King. All His servants had contacted a great debt of sin which they were unable to pay. In wonderful grace and compassion, The Lord paid the debt and granted full and free forgiveness. Now suppose one Christian wrongs another. When rebuked, he apologizes and asks for forgiveness. But the offended believer refuses. He himself has been forgiven millions of dollars, but won't forgive a few hundred. Will the King allow such behavior to go unpunished? Certainly not! The culprit will be chastened in this life and will suffer loss at the Judgment Seat of Christ." (Believer's Bible Commentary, William MacDonald, 1995)

The Pulpit Commentary comments, "'So likewise'. This points to the moral of the parable intended by Christ. It is not a lesson against ingratitude, but against unmercifulness, *"Blessed are the merciful: for they shall obtain mercy."* (Matthew 5:7). But want of charity makes a man incapable of retaining God's pardon. The Holy Spirit cannot abide in an unforgiving soul. *"My heavenly Father"*, He says, not "your": *"So likewise shall my heavenly Father do also unto you, if ye from your hearts forgive not everyone his brother their trespasses."* (Matthew 18:35) (Full quotation mine).

Not "our" but "My heavenly Father", the Father of Jesus Christ, the God of all mercies. He cannot join Himself in mention with such as are not children of God. "From your hearts". Forgiveness must be real, sincere, not pretended, nor merely outward. There must not only be no outward act of revenge, but no malice in the heart, no storing up of evil passions for future outlet as occasion may arise. The heart must be in harmony with the conduct and both must evidence a true spirit of charity. This alone enables one to continue in a state of grace and in reconciliation with God; this alone makes prayer acceptable; and we are assured that, as our heavenly Father requires us to forgive without limit, so His mercy is infinite and will be extended to us in a measure unbounded."

MY CHALLENGE

My greatest challenge in this whole study on forgiveness is found in the Book of Hosea. *"I will heal their backsliding, I will love them freely: for mine anger is turned away from him."* (Hosea 14:4)

Herein comes Ephesians 4:26 – 27

26 *Be ye angry, and sin not: let not the sun go*

*down upon your wrath:*

[27] *Neither give place to the devil.*

And the appeal from Jesus Christ Himself in Mark's gospel,

(Mark 11:25)

*And when ye stand praying, forgive, if ye have ought against any: that your Father also which is in heaven may forgive you your trespasses.*

And in Matthew's gospel,

(Matthew 5:11 – 12)

[11] *Blessed are ye, when men shall revile you, and persecute you, and shall say all manner of evil against you falsely, for my sake.*

[12] *Rejoice, and be exceeding glad: for great is your reward in heaven: for so persecuted they the prophets which were before you.*

In 1 Peter 2:21 – 23 we read,

[21] *For even hereunto were ye called: because Christ also suffered for us, leaving us an example, that ye should follow his steps:*

> [22] *Who did no sin, neither was guile found in his mouth:*
> [23] *Who, when he was reviled, reviled not again; when he suffered, he threatened not; but committed himself to him that judgeth righteously:*

Hebrews 12:1 – 3 states,

> [1] *Wherefore seeing we also are compassed about with so great a cloud of witnesses, let us lay aside every weight, and the sin which doth so easily beset us, and let us run with patience the race that is set before us,*
> [2] *Looking unto Jesus the author and finisher of our faith; Who for the joy that was set before him endured the cross, despising the shame, and is set down at the right hand of the throne of God.*
> [3] *For consider him that endured such contradiction of sinners against himself, lest ye be wearied and faint in your minds.*

**Let us start forgiving! And forgiving totally!!**

# CHAPTER 20

# THE BOOMERANG OF UNFORGIVENESS: SHYLOCK AND HIS POUND OF FLESH

Shakespeare's "Merchant of Venice" illustrates what Scripture says about unforgiveness. The Scriptures teach that the unmerciful, the unforgiving, the hard heart that cannot be begged, the heart insistent on revenge and tit for tat, shall lose out in the end.

Shylock, a money lender was one such example. Antonio, a merchant of Venice had borrowed money from him. The terms of payment or the bond stipulated that if the merchant defaulted, a "pound of flesh would be cut off from his chest" as payment for the principal and the interest. Unfortunately, and unexpectedly, Antonio suffered a calamity and as a result was unable to pay. Antonio and his friends went to Shylock to plead for mercy for the merchant, even offering to pay Shylock six times what was being owed in exchange for "the pound of flesh" but he refused. He was adamant.

Shylock was variously described by some of the dramatis personae as

I. "...a stony adversary, an inhuman wretch uncapable of pity, void and empty from any dram of mercy" (The Duke)
ii. "How shalt thou hope for mercy, rendering none?" (The Duke)
iii. "Can no prayers pierce thee?" (Gratiano)
iv. Portia (Antonio's lawyer) pleaded:
The quality of mercy is not strain'd,
It droppeth as the gentle rain from heaven
Upon the place beneath: it is twice blest;
It blesseth him that gives and him that takes:
'Tis mightiest in the mightiest: it becomes
The throned monarch better than his crown;
His sceptre shows the force of temporal power,
The attribute to awe and majesty,
Wherein doth sit the dread and fear of kings;
But mercy is above this sceptred sway;
It is enthroned in the hearts of kings,
It is an attribute to God himself;
And earthly power doth then show likest God's

When mercy seasons justice. Therefore, Jew,
Though justice be thy plea, consider this,
That, in the course of justice, none of us
Should see salvation: we do pray for mercy;
And that same prayer doth teach us all to render
The deeds of mercy. I have spoke thus much
To mitigate the justice of thy plea;
Which if thou follow, this strict court of Venice
Must needs give sentence 'gainst the merchant there.

"The quality of mercy is not strained – meaning, "mercy is not forced but given willingly." Psalms 130:3, *"If Thou Lord, shouldest mark iniquities, O Lord, who shall stand?"*

v. Shylock himself described his own heart, "... there is no power in the tongue of man to alter me, I stay here on my bond."

When no amount of pleading and begging could dissuade Shylock, the court granted Shylock permission to cut his "pound of flesh" off Antonio's chest but with this proviso: he was to "shed no blood nor cut off less or more but just a pound of flesh" and from the chest. "If thou cut more or less than a just pound, be it but so much as makes it light or heavy in the substance, or the division of the twentieth part of one poor scruple, nay, if the scale do turn but in the estimation of a hair, thou diest and all thy goods are confiscate."

It was at this point it dawned on Shylock that the game was up; he had lost everything and now was in danger of losing his own very life also. A hard hearted unforgiving Shylock at the end found himself on the begging side!

*"So likewise shall my heavenly Father do also unto you, if ye from your hearts forgive not everyone his brother their trespasses."* (Matthew 18:35)

So dear "Shylock" brethren, what lessons? – To learn to forgive or not to forgive?

Read God's plea in Proverbs 3:1-8

*[1]My son, forget not my law; but let thine heart keep my commandments:*
*[2]For length of days, and long life, and peace, shall they add to thee.*
*[3]Let not mercy and truth forsake thee: bind them about thy neck; write them upon the table of thine heart:*
*[4] So shalt thou find favour and good understanding in the sight of God and man.*
*[5]Trust in the Lord with all thine heart; and lean not unto thine own understanding.*
*[6] In all thy ways acknowledge him, and he shall direct thy paths.*
*[7]Be not wise in thine own eyes: fear the Lord, and depart from evil.*
*[8]It shall be health to thy navel, and marrow to thy bones.*

# CHAPTER 21

# CONCLUSION

"FORGIVENESS" has passed through **three** dispensational eras. It has passed through:

1. THE PRE-LAW DISPENSATION – when men avenged offenses beyond the offenses committed.
2. THE DISPENSATION OF THE LAW – When there was "equality of revenge", when men were not allowed to revenge beyond the offense committed and
3. THE DISPENSATION OF GRACE – where men are completely bared from revenge but encouraged to forgive instead and to leave vengeance to God.

HEART FORGIVENESS AND RELATIONSHIP

"Forgiveness" must be from the heart. It must be complete and total. We must forgive and restore the relationship; for if we say we have forgiven and do not relate or restore the strained relationship, we have not fully, truly forgiven.

WARNINGS ARE POSTED

Warnings are posted in this Dispensation of Grace which bars everyone from taking undue advantage of "grace". In Acts of the Apostles, it is posted:

> *"And the times of this ignorance God winked at; but now commandeth all men every where to repent:"* (Acts 17:30)

In Hebrews it is posted:
(Hebrews 2:1 – 3)

> [1] *Therefore* ***we ought to give the more earnest heed to the things which we have heard, lest at any time we should let them slip.***
> [2] ***For if the word spoken by angels was stedfast, and every transgression and disobedience received a just recompence of reward;***
> [3] *How shall we escape,* ***if we neglect*** *so great salvation; which at the first began to be spoken by the Lord, and was confirmed unto us by them that heard him;*

In the letter to the Corinthian Church, it is posted:

> *And having in readiness to avenge all disobedience...* (2 Corinthians 10:6)

In the epistle of Peter it is posted: *"And if the righteous scarcely be saved, where shall the ungodly and sinner appear?"* (in heaven or in hell?) "Scarcely" means, "only just, almost not."

In Saint Luke's Gospel, Jesus Himself warned,

> *Strive to enter in at the strait gate: for many, I say unto you, will seek to enter in, and shall not be able.* (Luke 13:24)

"Strive" means, "to try very hard to achieve".

FINAL ADVICE

My concluding advice is from the book of Jeremiah:

> *Thus saith the Lord, Stand ye in the ways, and see, and ask for the old paths, where is the good way, and walk therein, and ye shall find rest for your souls...* (Jeremiah 6:16)

Adam Clarke's explanation on this Verse is very lucid. "A traveller is going to a particular city. He comes to a place where the road divides into several paths; he is afraid of going astray. He stops short – endeavours to find out the right path; he cannot fix his choice. At last he sees another traveller; he inquires of him, gets proper directions – proceeds on his journey – arrives at the desired place – and reposes after his fatigue." (Adam Clarke's Commentary, 1972).

The Prophet Isaiah encourages, *"Learn to do well..."* (Isaiah 1:17)

Jesus concludes,

> *Take my yoke upon you, and learn of me; for I am meek and lowly in heart: and ye shall find rest unto your souls.* (Matthew 11:29)

ODE ON HEART FORGIVENESS OR FORGIVING FROM THE HEART

"Ode" means "a poem that speaks to a person or thing or celebrates a specific event." (Oxford Advanced Learners Dictionary)

(Philippians 4:8 )

> *Finally, brethren, whatsoever things are true, whatsoever things are honest, whatsoever things are just, whatsoever things are pure, whatsoever things are lovely, whatsoever things are of good report; if there be any virtue, and if there be any praise, THINK ON THESE THINGS.*

You also can forgive and have your own deliverance, healing and miracle. Therefore, you can sing this song of freedom:

> *I am delivered, praise the Lord*
> *I am delivered, by His blood*
> *Once I was bound by the chains of Satan but now*
> *I am delivered praise the Lord.*

# BOOKS BY
## APOSTLE & PST. (DR.) MRS.
# G. D. NUMBERE

### A Man And A Vision
**(A Biography Of Apostle Geoffrey D. Numbere)**

This book is a "must" for any person who desires to experience everything that God can do through a person wholly given over to His service. It is a "must" for every Pentecostal who seriously wonders if the age of miracles and divine healing really did pass away with the ending of the Apostolic Era. But especially for those aspiring to become Pentecostal leaders, this book, **A Man And A Vision** will inspire your faith and give you an honest hope that what God did in the Apostolic Church, He can and still does so today through those wholly committed to His service.

### Buying Into Another Man's Vision

Many a Mission or Ministry has failed because either the leader has not been called by God or was called not to head a Ministry but to buy into the vision of another. Besides, there are consequences on both the break-away leader and his/her followers. This book serves as a guide to many Christians to seek the mind of God to know the nature of their call and ensure God's blessings and fulfilment of their ministry.

### Greater Evangelism World Crusade: Landmarks In Her Vision And History (Third Edition)

Apostle G. D. Numbere who was miraculously born again on 11 May 1969, had a vision which gave birth to the Ministry of Greater Evangelism World Crusade on 9th September 1972. He had a vision and he ran with it. He shared the vision with others and those who dared to catch it ran with it. Over the years, many more have caught it and have run with it. Like Habakkuk, the vision is made "plain upon tables (in this book) that he may run that readeth it" (Habakkuk 2:2)

## Spiritual Foundations: Digging Deep

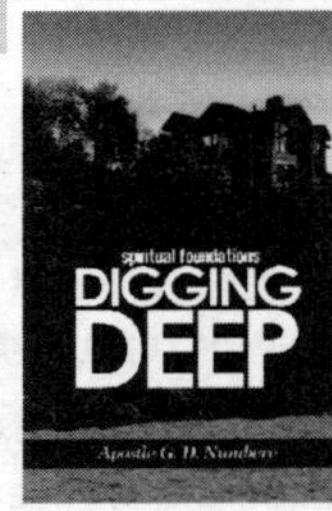


Digging Deep has nothing to do with the nominal Christian or the merely religious person. Digging Deep is a counsel to the born again Christian. A seed or a young plant will not grow to maturity or bear fruit if it is uprooted and replanted repeatedly. Nor will it grow and be firmly rooted if it is planted on a porous sandy soil. Digging Deep is an attempt to encourage Christians to lay a good solid foundation of faith.

## The Eagle Christian

In demonstrating boldness, forthrightness, tact, fidelity, cleanliness, thoroughness and dependability, the eagle exemplifies vintage Christian life. Apostle Numbere has in this book, effectively shown the way to rise above ordinariness and despondency by being what God intended us to be – **"Eagle Christians".**

## Unity Of The Brethren In The Local Church

In this book, Apostle Numbere and his wife, Pastor (Dr.) Nonyem, outline clearly and graphically, biblical principles on church nurture, growth and unity. They teach that Church growth is a building process which calls for maturity, care, diligence and much prayer. Also available in French.

## Word Killeth, Word Maketh Alive

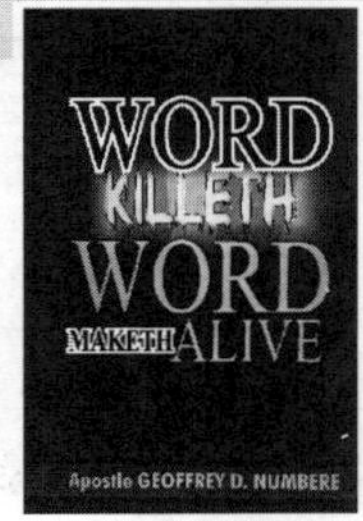


It is not only the words we speak, but also the names we give or bear that have effect on our lives. Have you ever thought about the meaning of the names you bear? This book is unique in that it does not just tell you the effects of bad words or names, but also tells you how to have victory whether you are a user or a victim. You will sure find it a nugget of gold as you come to realise that *"Life and Death are in the power of the tongue": in other words, "Word Killeth, Word Maketh Alive".*